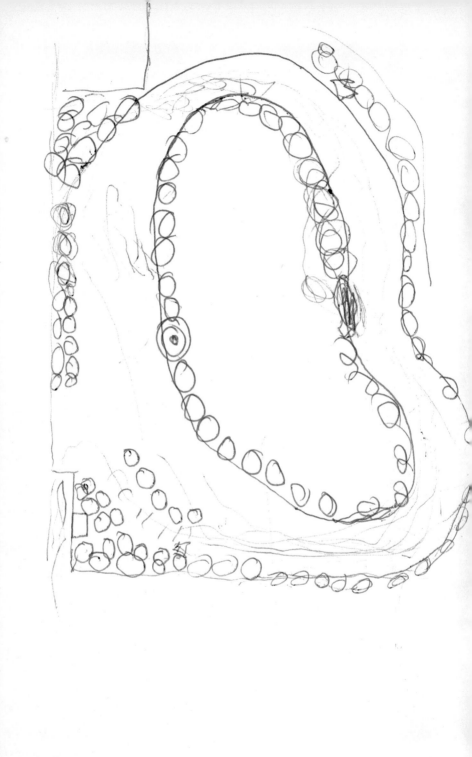

Dwight D. Eisenhower

The inspiring story of a distinguished American, including his West Point days as a cadet, his service as Supreme Commander of Allied ETO invasion forces, and his two terms as President.

by Malcolm Moos

Dwight D. Eisenhower

Illustrated with photographs

RANDOM HOUSE   NEW YORK

Grateful acknowledgment is made to:

Doubleday & Company, Inc. for permission to use on pages 51, 55-56, 63, 65-66, 70, 81, 88 and 105-106 quotations from *Crusade in Europe* by Dwight D. Eisenhower. Copyright, 1948, by Doubleday & Company, Inc.

Harper & Row, Publishers, Inc. for permission to use on pages 74 and 78 quotations from *Eisenhower: the Man and the Symbol* by John Gunther. Copyright, 1951, 1952, by John Gunther.

David McKay Company, Inc. for permission to use on pages 96-97 a quotation from Eisenhower's *Six Great Decisions* by General Walter Bedell Smith, published by Longmans, Green and Company (New York). Copyright © 1956 by Walter Bedell Smith; Copyright 1946 by the Curtis Publishing Co.

Prentice-Hall, Inc. for permission to use on page 125 a quotation from *Eisenhower Was My Boss* by Kay Summersby. Copyright, 1948, by Kay Summersby. Published by Prentice-Hall, Inc.

Simon and Schuster, Inc. for permission to use on page 100 a quotation from *My Three Years with Eisenhower* by Captain Harry C. Butcher. Copyright, 1946, by Harry C. Butcher.

Photograph credits: Brown Brothers, page 39 (top); Columbia University News Office, 134; Culver Pictures, 6, 39 (bottom), John Eisenhower, 44, 49; European Picture Service, 18; Monkmeyer Press Photo Service (by Jeffcoat), 8, 11, 23, 25, 31; Pix, 84, 101; United Press International, 16, 68, 126, 146, 153, 160, 163, 169; United States Air Force, 73, 117; United States Army, ii, 53, 61, 80, 92, 94; Wide World Photos, 34, 64, 77, 105, 110, 123, 130, 137, 139, 142.

Endpaper: U.S. Army

COVER: WIDE WORLD

MAPS: JEROME KUHL

Designed by Jane Byers

Library of Congress catalog card number: 64-12019

Contents

Maps

Dwight D. Eisenhower

"Bright . . . a Good Athlete . . . and Will Make Good"

On the warm sunny morning of June 2, 1911, a young man turned at the door of a cheerful, white-framed house to say good-by to his mother, his youngest brother and a small white dog named Flip. The mother was in tears, and the young man tried to comfort her. But it was an awkward moment. Finally even Flip joined the mourning. When the little dog threw his head back and began to bay and howl, the young man grabbed his bag and fled across a field. Perhaps he would find peace of mind in the dimly lit interior of a train.

His departure was not wholly unnoticed by his fellow

townsmen. On the same day the local newspaper, the Abilene *Daily Reflector,* carried a brief story:

> Dwight Eisenhower left today for West Point where he will join the Freshman class. . . . He is a bright young man and is a good athlete *and will make good.*

On this note, Dwight David Eisenhower, aged twenty, started out on the first leg of his journey—a journey that would eventually include fifty years of public service. During his lifetime he would serve as Supreme Commander of World War II Allied forces in Europe, president of Columbia University, Supreme Allied Commander of the North Atlantic Treaty Organization (NATO) and President of the United States.

Young Dwight Eisenhower's early, formative years were spent on the rolling plains of Kansas. His father, David Jacob Eisenhower, was third among seven sons in a family whose ancestors had come to Pennsylvania from Bavaria sometime before 1750. Dwight's mother, Ida Stover, was descended from Swiss emigrants who became settlers in the Shenandoah Valley of Virginia about the same time.

In 1878 Dwight's grandfather and father moved from Pennsylvania to Kansas, settling near Abilene. His mother came to Kansas with her brothers four years later. While Ida and David were both students at Lane University in Lecompton, Kansas, they met and married. For a time thereafter, David operated a general merchandise store at Hope, Kansas, but he fell upon hard times. During the drought of 1888 the business failed, and Ida and David moved to Denison, Texas. Here their third son, David Dwight, was born on October 14, 1890. (Later he was to reverse the order of these names to Dwight David.) The following spring they returned to Kansas to settle permanently, this time in the historic frontier town of Abilene.

The Eisenhowers' home in Abilene was, to use the familiar cliché, on the wrong side of the tracks. Later on, Dwight reported that this had never bothered him too much, except when he had to take home-grown vegetables to the north side to sell. Here the well-to-do housewives would accept only the most perfect ears of corn, and frequently they haggled over pennies.

At least once a year the north and south sides of town had a fight, usually with each side represented by one boy. When he was just thirteen, young Dwight represented the south side in a fight in which he was decidedly the underdog. Small and slender for his age, he was also considered somewhat slow as an athlete. Nevertheless the fight lasted two hours and ended in a draw, putting Dwight out of commission for three days. In the end each contestant acknowledged that he had been unable to beat the other.

Altogether there were six boys in the Eisenhower family—Arthur, Edgar, Dwight, and three younger brothers, Roy, Earl, and Milton. Another boy, Paul, died in infancy. The youngest—Milton—narrowly escaped death in the days before antibiotics when he came down with a severe case of scarlet fever. During the long

David and Ida Eisenhower with their six sons (1900). Back row, left to right: Dwight, Edgar, Earl, Arthur and Roy; front row: Milton.

period of Milton's convalescence, Dwight showed a fierce determination to protect his small brother from anyone who tried to pick on him. Milton's fragile health during childhood and his position as the youngest in the family established a close bond between the two. This bond was to grow warmer over the years and lead to the frequent presumption that Milt must be Dwight's favorite brother.

All six brothers grew up in a highly religious atmosphere. The family owned three Bibles—one in Greek for the father, a German Bible with the family names in it, and the King James version for the mother and the boys. At least one night a week was set aside for Bible

reading, though frequently it was read with the same
regularity that daily prayers were recited. Both
Dwight's father and mother could quote at length from
the Bible.

The Eisenhower family belonged to a Mennonite
sect called the Church of the River Brethren. The
members wore dark, old-fashioned-looking clothes, and
their beliefs stressed simplicity, self-reliance, duty,
responsibility, and great hatred of war and violence.
Pacifism was very much a central part of the River
Brethren faith, and his early church teaching undoubt-
edly left its mark on Dwight. In later years his passion
for peace led the French to symbolize this trait by
calling him a "peace general."

Throughout childhood, religion was an intensely live
part of Dwight's life. He believed in it and accepted
happily the belief that all would be well in this world
if each man would accept the "cards he had been
dealt and play them to the best of his ability."

In the comfortable but simple eight-room house
where Dwight grew up, all six brothers took an active
hand in the family chores. Dwight was poor at fire-
building because he couldn't get up early in the
morning. (This report invariably brings smiles to his
Army and White House staffs of later years. They
recall with groans his early rising habits.) On Sundays
the Eisenhower boys did all the chores including the
cooking of meals. Their mother would have been
horrified to know that they kneaded pie dough by
tossing it back and forth, and used the same technique

The Eisenhower family home in Abilene.

when attacking a mound of dishes.

Like all boys, the Eisenhowers loved to fight mock Wild West battles. During the 1860s Texas cattlemen had driven their herds northward to the Kansas railroads. At that time Abilene was on the edge of the American frontier. It was the last stop on the railroad being built across the continent, and the last stop on the Old Chisholm Trail. During the summer months thousands of longhorn steers were driven north from San Antonio over this famous cattle trail. After arrival in Abilene, they were sold and shipped by rail to Chicago.

The cowboys who drove the cattle up the long dusty trail from Texas were a high-spirited group. They had to be. Riding trail with a herd of longhorns from Texas to Abilene was rugged work and put the

men under constant strain for weeks. Once the cowboys reached Abilene and had their cattle safely
loaded on trains, they felt the urge to blow off a little
steam. They swaggered about the town, shooting off
their guns whenever it pleased them.

Something had to be done to establish law and
order, and finally the townsmen decided to hire a
town marshal. His name was Tom Smith. A quiet
man, who rode a large gray horse called Silverheels,
Smith could shoot straight to the mark and draw with
the best of them. His first act was to disarm the
cowboys. This he did by making them leave their
guns with the proprietors of any establishment they
entered. Of course the task was far from simple,
and in the beginning he had to knock a few heads
together to enforce his rules. But Tom Smith prevailed,
and Abilene became a far better place in which to live.

The lesson taught by Marshal Tom Smith lingered
on, and it was not lost on the Eisenhower boys.
In fact that lesson—the development of a sense of
orderly progress, the idea that there is a way to
establish justice and freedom in the world—sustained
Eisenhower over the years. In the small cemetery in
Abilene, his parents lie close to the grave of Tom
Smith. Whenever Dwight Eisenhower visits this plot,
an accompanying friend is certain to hear the story
of the peerless marshal who brought peace to Abilene.

By the time Dwight was born, the cattle drives had
moved farther west, but Abilene was still a town filled
with the exciting memory of the Old West. And the

Eisenhower boys loved to reënact the adventures of the famous Chisholm Trail.

While still in his early teens Dwight was running home from school one day when he stumbled and fell, skinning his left knee. A serious infection developed. When blood poisoning set in, the doctor wanted to amputate his leg, but Dwight refused. Before he became delirious, he made his brother Ed promise not to let them operate. Ed stayed by his bed or slept in front of his door for days and nights until—miraculously—Dwight began to recover. He walked out of the bedroom on both his legs.

Dwight finished the first eight grades at the Lincoln and Garfield grammar schools, and then went to the Abilene High School. His marks were well above average. In his senior year they were particularly high in history and math—an impressive performance considering his heavy outside work load.

Both Dwight and Ed worked at the same town creamery where their father was employed as night watchman and mechanic. They alternated evenings in the engine room. By now they were well aware of the responsibility they bore for advancing their own education. When Dwight was ten his mother had told him: "If you want an education, go out and get it." All the boys took to heart this crisp warning of their mother, who was fond of such phrases as "sink or swim" and "survive or perish."

Despite his job Dwight put a great deal of energy

Young Dwight Eisenhower (third from left in the back row) and the 1909 Abilene High School football team.

into his high school life. He worked hard both at his studies and in athletics, and he left behind him a wealth of legends and some contradictions. One of his best friends was John "Six" MacDonell, a star baseball player who later became a professional. In one football game, when the opposing team roughed up little Six, Dwight is said to have gone wild. One report credited him with knocking out four opponents; another said he had done a thorough job of roughing them up.

Dwight's friend Six had a part-time job in the office of the Dickinson County *News*, and he introduced Dwight to Joe W. Howe, the editor and publisher of this weekly Abilene newspaper. Here in the cluttered surroundings of a small country newspaper office Dwight delved into the editor's library, and for the first time did some really serious spare-time reading. One book in particular—a life of Hannibal—fascinated him. He was especially interested in its account of the Punic wars. Joe Howe enjoyed having a gang of boys around the office, and he even fixed up a special room where they practiced boxing.

In 1909 Dwight graduated from high school. He and Edgar were in the same graduating class since Ed had left school for a year to work in order to help the family finances. *Helianthus*, the senior yearbook, went wide of the mark in prophesying their futures—but only in picking the wrong brother for the right job. It predicted that Edgar would serve two terms as President of the United States; Dwight would be a professor of history at Yale University. By this time, incidentally, the two brothers were commonly known as "Big Ike" and "Little Ike."

They decided that they would alternate work with college, so that one of them would lend a financial hand while the other studied. Ed was the first to go off to school because he knew what he wanted to do—study law. (Dwight was still the little one.) While Ed studied at the University of Michigan, Dwight remained behind in Abilene, working. He returned to the creamery, sent money to Ed, and dated his first girl. But soon he became restless with his work, felt he was drifting, and grew eager for a change.

About this time he met Everett E. Hazlett, Jr., who was more frequently called "Swede." They gradually became fast friends. Swede hailed from the well-to-do north side of Abilene and yearned to be admitted to Annapolis, even though he had flunked the entrance exams on the first try. Soon he had Dwight interested in the possibility, too. They began studying together every afternoon, before Dwight went off to the creamery where he worked from 6:00 P.M. to 6:00 A.M. Early that autumn, with the encouragement of several prominent Abilene civic figures, he began corresponding with Senator Joseph L. Bristow.

Senator Bristow was an unusually able congressman, not as widely known, perhaps, as his record deserved. In a day when few senators gave any thought to competitive examinations for appointments to the United States Naval or Military academies at Annapolis and West Point—usually they appointed sons of friends— Senator Bristow believed in giving examinations as one indication of merit.

On October 4th, 1910, Dwight went to Topeka to take exams for both West Point and Annapolis, hoping, of course, for appointment to Annapolis. He scored first among all contestants for appointment to the Naval Academy, and second for West Point. Then came a sad moment. He suddenly discovered that he was too old for Annapolis and felt he must disqualify himself.

But help came from an unexpected quarter. The boy who ranked first for West Point dropped out. Senator Bristow appointed young Ike, and so a land-locked Middle Westerner who yearned for the sea was sent to the service academy on the Hudson instead of the Severn.

Ike's parents looked upon this development with considerable distress. Anything to do with the prepara-tion for war ran contrary to their most sacred beliefs. His mother cried when she learned of his appointment, though she expressed no surprise that he had placed so high in the examinations.

Ike made no attempt to justify his decision to enter West Point on moral grounds, which he knew his mother would find distasteful. But he did uphold his decision on the grounds that a career at the Military Academy offered a grand opportunity for a free education. Besides, he said, it didn't commit him for life. Gradually his parents became more reconciled to the idea.

Meantime, he returned to Abilene High as a graduate student and played tackle on the football team for the rest of the season. In the spring of 1911 he passed his entrance exams to West Point, and in June the time came to say good-by.

Duty, Honor, Country

Any thoughts of leading a carefree, casual life disappeared when Ike caught his first glimpse of West Point. The granite walls of the brooding, fortress-like buildings and the first assemblage of the cadets cast a spell over him that he retained throughout life. For forty years the army was to be the center of the universe for Dwight D. Eisenhower.

His unflagging optimism served him well at West Point, and he was even able to buck up the spirits of cadets who became downcast or disenchanted. He adjusted quickly to the new environment and won his highest grades during his plebe year. In a class

Cadet Eisenhower studies in his West Point quarters.

of 212, he stood 57th. His best grades were in English, where he stood 10th in his class, and in history, where he was 39th. He was able to turn out an English essay in a half-hour, much to the despair of his roommate. In all written work he liked brevity and tight organization. He persisted in believing that anything worth saying could be said in a page. If it couldn't, it wasn't worth saying.

Never one to pass up a little fun now and then, Dwight took quite a few reckless chances and acquired a generous number of demerits for breaking the Academy's strict regulations. Once when summoned by upper classmen to turn up in a dress coat, he did—but without trousers. Nobody, he insisted, had mentioned pants!

Football won Dwight's heart as a sport, and he soon gave promise of becoming a star player. He played a bruising, hard-blocking game, but with strict regard for the ground rules. And he played against some of football's immortals. Perhaps his greatest game was against the Carlisle Indians during his second year.

Jim Thorpe, well known as one of the world's greatest all-around athletes, was playing for Carlisle in that game. He proved too much for the cadets. The West Point team lost, with a score of six to twenty-seven, and Dwight emerged from the hard-fought grid-iron contest with a badly sprained knee. In his next game he compounded the injury by breaking the knee. He was forced to retire from the gridiron permanently— but not as a spectator. Probably no award or decoration ever pleased him more than the gold football he received fifty years later when he was placed in the hall of fame of the nation's pigskin heroes.

When Dwight left the hospital the doctor warned him not to put any more weight on his knee than absolutely necessary. He specifically forbade the cadet to mount or dismount during riding drill. But the riding instructor was unsympathetic, and one day he accused Dwight of pretending to be more badly injured than he really was. Dwight was so angry that he spent most of the afternoon mounting and dismounting. This strain did further injury to his knee, and by the end of the session he had to be almost

carried to the chief surgeon, Dr. Charles Keller. The knee injury not only closed Dwight's football career, but came close to ending his army career as well. Dr. Keller, the much loved West Point physician, had to stretch a point in the physical requirements to graduate him.

Dwight finished his second year as 81st in a class that had dwindled to 177. During the summer of 1913, he received his first thirty-day furlough and made a surprise visit home. Everyone was in bed when he arrived, but the faithful Flip shot across the lawn to welcome him. The little dog barked furiously while Ike chased from room to room to make sure nothing had been changed. This was a practice he invariably followed on subsequent visits.

Spring of 1915—Dwight's last year at West Point— brought a definite change of climate to the Academy. World War I, which had started in August of 1914, had bogged down into a long-drawn-out trench warfare after the German armies failed to bring about the swift fall of Paris. The United States, under President Woodrow Wilson's leadership, was still attempting to stay neutral. But on May 7, 1915, a sudden tragedy in the North Atlantic jolted American neutrality. A German U-boat, lurking beneath the surface off the coast of Ireland, sank the *Lusitania* with a loss of 1,198 lives. Among the dead on the British passenger ship were 128 Americans. The tension generated by this tragic event made it increasingly clear that the

At the Academy Dwight gave promise of becoming a star football player.

United States would be drawn into World War I. The end of an era of security had come.

On June 12, 1915, Dwight graduated from West Point, placing 61st out of 164. He stood in the first third of his class academically and in the lowest third in conduct. Commissioned a second lieutenant in the infantry, he set as his ultimate goal the rank of colonel. It was not lack of ambition that prompted him to set this ceiling. He simply thought he would be unable to climb to a higher rank because of his age. He was almost twenty-five.

The Hinge of Happiness and Tragedy

Mid-September found Lieutenant Eisenhower in Galveston, Texas, where he had gone to join the 19th Infantry. There he discovered that a flood had forced his regiment to move on to Fort Sam Houston at San Antonio. Near by was one of the nation's most famous military shrines—the Alamo.

In San Antonio Lieutenant Eisenhower met, and became enchanted with, Mamie Geneva Doud. She was a briskly enthusiastic and popular young woman, the daughter of a prominent and wealthy Denver family. Mamie quickly became his towering interest. On St. Valentine's Day, 1916, Ike gave her his class ring, and on July 1st they were married at her mother's home in Denver. That same day he was promoted to the rank of first lieutenant.

After a brief but extremely happy honeymoon furlough in Abilene, Ike and Mamie moved into a tiny apartment at Fort Sam Houston. Initially he was put in charge of a military police detail—an assignment that meant patrolling some of the toughest areas of San Antonio. Twice he was shot at—once by an unknown assailant and once, at point-blank range, by a drunken private who luckily had exceptionally bad aim. Both shots failed to hit their mark. Lieutenant Eisenhower also spent considerable time on detached service at Camp Wilson, where he helped train the National Guardsmen who were patrolling the Mexican border to prevent surprise raids by the Mexican bandit chieftain, Pancho Villa.

In the spring of 1917 he became regimental supply officer for the 57th Infantry at Leon Springs, and on April 6, 1917, the United States finally entered World War I. America's entry into the war brought a new sense of urgency to the professional soldier. For a time Ike even considered applying for a transfer to the Air Corps, but Mamie argued against it. Instead, on September 18, 1917, he assumed new responsibilities as an instructor at the Officers' Training Camp at Fort Oglethorpe, Georgia. He had now attained the rank of captain. Mamie remained in Texas and six days

Lieutenant and Mrs. Dwight D. Eisenhower on their wedding day.

later, on September 24th, their first child—Doud Dwight
—was born. The approaching birth of this child had
been the reason for Mamie's strong opposition to the
Air Corps and its flimsy planes.

In December Ike was transferred to Fort Leavenworth, where he was an instructor in the Army Service
Schools. Here he also studied in one of the pioneer
tank schools, analyzing the European armies' experi-
mental uses of tanks in the opening phases of World
War I. Two months later he was assigned to the 65th
Battalion Engineers at Camp Meade, Maryland.

The next move—one which would prove of major
importance—came in March of 1918. He was sent to
Camp Colt at Gettysburg, Pennsylvania, to command
the tank training center. Here Mrs. Eisenhower and
their six-month-old son were able to join him.

The irony of what Captain Eisenhower found at
Camp Colt is a little like that of the peacetime draft
conditions just prior to America's entry into World War
II, when men drilled with broomsticks because there
were no rifles for training use. Camp Colt had
thousands of men, but no tanks. The camp finally
received one tank—a French model—but that was all.

Despite such meager equipment, Ike's soaring spirits
never flagged. He put into effect a training program
which proved remarkably practical considering the
limitations of equipment. In recognition of his excellent
work, he was promoted in midsummer to the rank of
temporary major. And on October 14th—his twenty-
eighth birthday—he was raised to the rank of tem-

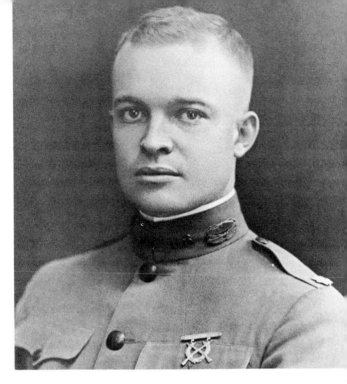

A picture of Colonel Eisenhower taken during World War I.

porary lieutenant colonel. These promotions, of course, were partly accelerated by the fact that the United States was at war. But they were even more the result of his tireless efforts as camp commander.

Ten years later he was awarded the Distinguished Service Medal for his "unusual zeal, foresight, and marked administrative ability [at Camp Colt] in the organization, training, and preparation for overseas service of technical troops of the Tank Corps." Such an honor was rarely given at that time for services within the continental borders of the United States.

The next obvious step, of course—and one he deeply

yearned for—was to get into the scrap and go overseas. He was delighted in November when he learned
he was to be sent to Fort Dix, New Jersey, the
embarkation point for troops destined to go overseas.
But on November 11th the Armistice finally silenced
the guns in Western Europe and the disappointed
colonel never left New Jersey. Instead he was soon
posted to Fort Benning, Georgia, a famed infantry
training post. By March, 1919, he was back at Camp
Meade, serving first as an executive officer and later
as commander of successive heavy-tank battalions.
Once again his wife and son were able to join him.

In a dull postwar era the Camp Meade assignment
proved fascinating. The tank was a new weapon, but
the lessons learned from the limited use of armored,
mechanized weapons in World War I already indicated
that the day of the romantic cavalry troops was over.
In the future, snorting steel monsters that mounted
cannons instead of men with sabers and rifles would
take the field against the enemy. Men even talked of
radio control for tanks, but such dreams were quickly
dismissed. The tanks were still so small and the
primitive radio instruments so huge that a radio tank
in 1919 would have had space for little more than
a pair of pistols.

During the postwar period Eisenhower met a fellow
officer who was to have a big influence on his life—
Lieutenant Colonel George S. Patton, Jr. Patton had
served as commander of a tank brigade in France,
where he had exhibited tremendous personal courage

and bravery. The two men shared a mutual interest in sports and history, and they went riding together almost every day. They discussed military theory endlessly and agreed the army of the future must be mechanized.

It was George Patton who introduced Eisenhower to Brigadier General Fox Conner, a man destined to play an important part in Ike's future. Conner had served in France during World War I with the operations section of the General Staff of the American Expeditionary Forces. He was a man of vast experience and a keen student of military science. Already he foresaw that the First World War had been just a prelude to another, larger conflict. There would be no security, he said, and Eisenhower should prepare himself for the conflict that would surely come in twenty or thirty years. Conner impressed upon the young officer the value of reading the classics of warfare incessantly and mastering their lessons.

This phase of Ike's career was not entirely a happy one, however. In the fall of 1919 his application to the Infantry School was rejected by his superior officer. Attendance at the school was necessary if he hoped to go on to the Command and General Staff School at Leavenworth, so the rejection seemed to close the door to any hopes he had for eventual promotion to the General Staff. To ease his disappointment he attended the Infantry Tank School at Camp Meade.

Then in July of 1920 he lost his temporary war rank of lieutenant colonel, reverting to his permanent rank of captain. Although he was soon promoted again to major, he feared his age would prevent his ever winning the rank of full colonel.

Close on the heels of these setbacks came perhaps the most severe blow of his entire life. Scarlet fever, the disease that had almost taken the life of Ike's favorite brother, Milton, in infancy, struck his son, Doud Dwight. The little boy died on January 2, 1921, at the age of three years and three months.

Forty years later, after Mr. Eisenhower had twice served as President of the United States, he was working furiously on one of several drafts of his farewell address, just before leaving the White House. The author of this book was working with him. Suddenly the President asked if I had seen a particular phase of the war. No, I answered, explaining that I had been in the ROTC but was rejected for active service because of physical infirmities resulting from scarlet fever. He nodded, then walked to the east door of the beautiful oval office and stood looking out at the White House lawn and elipse beyond for several minutes. No further words were spoken. I felt it was time to leave.

"Be Ready ... Make No Move ...
Don't Even Breathe"

Eisenhower graduated from the tank school early in
1921, and was put in command of the 301st Tank
Battalion. A year later he went off to Panama as
executive officer to General Fox Conner, who had
especially requested him for the post. A new dimension
in warfare—air power—was posing difficult problems
for the Canal Zone. How could the Army protect the
canal from air attack and keep the locks in working
order to ensure passage for Navy vessels? Major
Eisenhower's mission was to help develop new and
adequate defense plans.

Mamie accompanied him on this assignment, and

29

the porch of their home quickly became the center of a lively social life. All newcomers in the Canal Zone were instructed not to kill bats because the bats ate malarial mosquitoes. But Mamie had no intention of sharing a house with a bat. When one flew into the bedroom she told Ike he had to kill it. He protested, saying it was against the law, but obliged obediently with great swishes of his saber.

In Panama Eisenhower formed a warm, lasting friendship with General Conner, who liked and admired him tremendously. One day the General was seeing to it that an old horse was properly shod. Just as the first shoe was being fitted, the unpredictable nag heaved forward, jabbing her nose into the General's stomach. Promptly Conner tumbled backward through a low window and into a huge tub of water directly beneath it. A young aide dashed frantically to the rescue as General Conner roared, "Don't you tell Eisenhower about this!"

In Panama, Ike's main goal was to prepare himself for the Command and General Staff School, if the opportunity ever came. He set up a study on the second floor of his house and spent long hours there with books of military history and science.

Meanwhile, Mrs. Eisenhower returned to her home in Denver where a second son, John Sheldon Doud Eisenhower, was born in August, 1922. As always, an immense loneliness descended upon Ike when he was separated from his family. He had to have someone dear close at hand, and when this was impossible during World War II, he acquired a scottie for companionship in his headquarters.

That fall a joyous sight awaited him as a gray transport edged into dock. Down the gangplank came a beaming Mamie with a three-month-old bundle tucked in her arms. The family was together again.

During the winter the reappearance of an old friend also added to Ike's happiness. Swede Hazlett, his old Abilene companion who had gone to Annapolis, phoned from the submarine base at Coco Solo to say that he would be laid up for several weeks with a burned-out motor. "Come up!" yelled Ike, which Swede did at

John Sheldon Doud Eisenhower (at the age of 2½) with his mother.

once. The two of them had a wonderful time exchanging news and renewing old activities. Later Ike took his first submarine ride with Swede. Although he was entranced by the experience of submerging, he knew he wouldn't want to change the service he had entered. Fate had directed him correctly to West Point instead of to Annapolis.

During Ike's stay in Panama, he spent many an evening with General Conner, talking far into the night. Even as the disarmament treaties were being ratified, Conner foresaw another war—and a terrible one—within fifteen or, at the most, twenty years. He correctly saw that a brilliantly staffed German army, even if limited by the Treaty of Versailles to one hundred thousand men, could form the nucleus of a future massive war machine. And to the east, he felt that the growing spirit of militarism in Japan could lead only to an imperialist power grab exploding into war. Conner also believed that Germany and Japan would very likely combine against England, France and the United States, with the possibility that even Russia might be with them.

What troubled Conner most was the floppy indifference in America toward world affairs and the urgent need to protect the very lifeline of the nation's security. So little time remained to prepare for the war that would surely come sooner than anyone could imagine.

"Young men, and you in particular," he would say to Ike, "have the qualities that will be urgently in demand." He was determined to use all his influence to get Eisenhower into the Command and General Staff School as soon as possible.

The major defensive plans for Panama were finally completed, however, and the Army ordered Major Eisenhower to return to the United States in September of 1924. Although his talks and friendship with Fox Conner had fired him with an evangelical zeal to reach Command and General Staff School, the Army had other plans. He was sent to Baltimore to act as a recreation officer for the Third Corps Area. Since this involved football coaching, he made no complaint. After all, he loved the game. He did eventually request a transfer to Fort Logan, Colorado, as recruiting officer, and this was granted. The move meant that they would be close to Mamie's family in nearby Denver.

All the while Conner kept counseling Ike with one hand, telling him not to despair. With the other hand he worked feverishly behind the scenes with the Army's top brass, persuading them to overlook the fact that Ike had not attended Infantry School. It was a supreme demonstration of his faith in Major Ike.

Finally a cryptic telegram arrived:

> BE READY . . . MAKE NO MOVE . . . DON'T
> EVEN BREATHE
>
> FOX CONNER

Conner's fierce faith in Eisenhower was amply justified. At Fort Leavenworth, Kansas, Ike worked hard and sprinted to the head of his class. Upon completion of the course he stood first in a class of

Major Dwight D. Eisenhower of the American Battle Monuments Commission.

275, a performance that put him high on the General Staff Corps Eligible List. Even this brilliant showing, however, did not make him leapfrog ahead in rank. He remained a major for a long time.

From 1927 to 1929 Eisenhower put in a tour of duty with the American Battle Monuments Commission. The commission, headed by General John J.

Pershing, had been collecting material for a guide to the American battlefields in France. The first portion of the work was carried out in Washington. Then in 1928 Eisenhower was sent to France, where he could study the terrain of Europe at first hand, from the Bay of Biscayne to the River Rhine. He took full advantage of this unique opportunity, mastering the details of every road, town and topographical feature of the entire area. At the same time he accumulated a vast store of information about America's military role in the First World War. The knowledge he soaked up was of inestimable value to him when he was planning for the invasion of Europe in 1944.

In part, this valuable experience must be credited to Mamie. It was she who encouraged Ike to make the trip to Europe for the Battle Monuments Commission. In fact she and John accompanied him there. This was only the second time that she had attempted to influence a decision affecting his career. The other episode had occurred when she talked him out of trying to transfer to the Air Corps.

The Eisenhowers returned to the States in September of 1929, and two months later Ike became assistant executive in the office of the assistant secretary of war. For three years in this assignment he concentrated on problems of military supply in case of war—analyzing sources of supply and transport and labor-procurement problems. He was working much of the time directly with industry in a difficult and complex administrative job.

In 1930 General Douglas MacArthur became Chief of Staff, and in February of 1933 Ike joined Mac-Arthur as his senior aide. It was a time of deepening depression and severe cutbacks that reduced the Army budget to bare subsistence levels. Yet both domestic and international events were churning away in a dangerously explosive series of crises. For the next thirty years Dwight Eisenhower would have no relief from crisis.

West to the Philippines

It is difficult to recreate the somber character of the early 1930s. They brought harrowing experiences to the millions who suffered unemployment and the hundreds of thousands who lost their homes through foreclosures. Thousands of others were uprooted from their farms by crop failures, depressed farm prices and the great drought and dust storms of the period.

For the professional soldier, the early thirties brought nightmarish worries. At home a tragic bonus march on the nation's Capitol brought the army to the dangerous edge of politics. The bonus law of 1924 had provided World War I veterans with certificates for bonuses payable in 1945. Because of the depression, veterans began demanding immediate payment. Large numbers of them decided that, if they marched upon Washington, Congress would be frightened into passing a bill that would meet their demand. In June, 1932, approximately 15,000 veterans of World War I began converging upon the capital from all sections of the country. Straggling into Washington without funds, they spilled into an encampment that soon became an eyesore of shanties and impoverished humanity. It also posed a menace to the public health.

Finally an order came to the Chief of Staff from President Herbert C. Hoover to clear out the bonus marchers with troops, but to make certain that no one was killed. MacArthur himself took on this most sensitive assignment, one which he carried out without incident in one of the sad hours of the nation's history. Nevertheless, there was severe criticism of the Army's part in the crisis.

With their forces stripped down to 118,000 men and involved in such unpopular assignments as evicting bonus marchers, the Army leaders could not fail to be uneasy about the gathering storm abroad. In 1931 the Japanese moved in to take the whole of Manchuria from China. Then early in 1933, Adolf Hitler and his Nazi party came to power in Germany and simultaneously began promoting a fanatical nationalism and an intensive rearmament program. In eastern Europe, the Soviet Union had a standing army of one million men.

In addition to the general domestic and international

General Douglas MacArthur (left) and his senior aide, Major Eisenhower, during the Bonus Army crisis.

The bonus marchers gather for a rally in Washington.

difficulties, a strong peace offensive was rapidly gaining momentum in America. Although much of this peace movement was animated by noble impulses and men of good faith, it was most frustrating to men gravely concerned by the inadequacy of American defenses. Huge peace strikes were organized at many land-grant universities by way of protesting and abolishing compulsory military training. At Princeton the protest found expression in the founding of the first chapter of an organization known as the Veterans for Future Wars. This group demanded immediate bonuses and other special considerations to all members before they went into the Army or set out for actual fighting.

In this atmosphere of bewildering domestic upheaval and international tension, Eisenhower began his close association with General MacArthur. At the latter's specific request, Ike moved into an office immediately adjacent to the General.

MacArthur, a brilliant, romantic figure, with a flair for the dramatic and theatrical, had set a record for achievement during his West Point days. He was both the highest ranking cadet in his class and the top man in his studies. As Chief of Staff, he was quickly impressed with the talents of his new aide. Eisenhower put a new verve into the reports of the Chief of Staff. They were clearly organized, concisely stated, and they contained frequent references to some of the great military leaders of the past. He set forth a well-defined case for military preparedness and a compact but well-equipped regular army back-stopped by an adequate, trained reserve. And not only did Eisenhower prove himself technically proficient in the preparation of staff reports, but he also showed that he had a sensitive grasp of public relations.. In short, he made it abundantly clear to his military superiors as well as to certain congressmen that he could do things well with both hands.

In 1934, Congress passed the Tydings-McDuffie Act, which provided for the granting of full independence to the Philippines after a ten-year period. Because of the islands' strategic position in the Pacific, it was imperative that during this ten-year period their defenses be greatly bolstered. MacArthur, who was finishing his tour of duty as Chief of Staff in 1935, was asked to become chief military adviser to the Philippines. Immediately he asked Eisenhower to become his assistant. He had already dictated the following letter, expressing his high regard for the Major's work:

> You were retained by the Secretary of War, and later by myself, on critically important duties in the Department long past the duration of ordinary staff tours, solely because of your success in performing difficult tasks whose accomplishment required a comprehensive grasp of the military profession in all its principal phases, as well as analytical thought and forceful expression. Through all these years I have been impressed by the cheerful and efficient devotion of your best efforts to confining, difficult and often strenuous duties, in spite of the fact that your own personal desires involved a return to troop command and other physically active phases of Army life, for

which your characteristics so well qualify you.

In this connection I should like to point out to you that your unusual experience in the Department will be of no less future value to you as a commander than as a staff officer, since all problems presented to you were necessarily solved from the viewpoint of the High Command . . . The numbers of personal requests for your services brought to me by heads of many of the Army's principal activities during the past few years furnish convincing proof of the reputation you have established as an outstanding soldier. I can say no more than that this reputation coincides exactly with my own judgment.

The chance to serve in the Commonwealth appealed to Eisenhower. He left for the Philippines in the fall of 1935 as the assistant military adviser to the Commonwealth, a post he held for four years. His first challenge was to help draw up the National Defense Act, which among other things provided for a citizens' military training program and an adequate defense system. Eisenhower also spent much of his time helping to found and develop a military academy at Baguio. He personally selected the site, high up at an altitude of 5,000 feet, where it was both cool and dry. And he was involved in working out the defense strategy used so tenaciously against the Japanese landing forces just a few years later on the Bataan peninsula.

Not unexpectedly, he met formidable obstacles in getting the work started. Both political and personal intrigue created difficult moments. Moreover, funds were scanty in the infant commonwealth. For instance,

Eisenhower wanted to secure 400,000 old Enfield rifles from the United States. He had arranged to purchase them for a very inexpensive figure, but his request was turned down. Fortunately 100,000 were finally sent in response to his efforts; they were used with major effect on Bataan five years later.

Ike's personal contact with the Filipinos was a source of lasting satisfaction. He was sympathetic and frank with them, and they trusted him in return. He had always admired the Philippine Scouts when they served in the United States Army, and now he came to know thousands of additional young men eager to prove their worth as soldiers of the young commonwealth.

Eisenhower had been in the Philippines for a full year before his wife arrived with John in the fall of 1936. He and John, who was now fourteen, became devoted companions. Eisenhower had long conversations with his son each morning while shaving. These sessions touched on every conceivable subject from sports to the question of smoking and drinking. The father's army experience gave him a down-to-earth approach to these typical boyhood problems. It was while they were living in Manila that John decided he wanted to attend West Point.

One day Eisenhower flew to Baguio to enroll John in a special school there. That afternoon, as the pilot prepared to fly him back, they were compelled to delay their take-off because the cross wind on the narrow strip made it hazardous. Finally they grew impatient—Ike had a dinner date—and took off. But the plane barely

Ike sits beside his plane after a flight to northern Luzon.

survived the take-off. The pilot battled for altitude,
trying first one valley and then another. Finally he
turned back to yell, "We're not going to make it." But
at the last minute the plane miraculously lifted. The
wheels just grazed the tips of the pine trees.

Undaunted, Ike now set out to do what he had long
ago set his heart on—to learn to fly. He took flying
lessons regularly, and became so excited with his hobby
that he even "practiced" at the dinner table, where he
simulated the controls with the silverware.

He took his first solo flight in a two-seater trainer.
To provide ballast a sandbag was placed in the rear
cockpit, but the dual controls were not removed. Ike
climbed to four thousand feet and went through several
maneuvers ending with a couple of loop-the-loops.

Coming out of the second loop, he suddenly found the stick was jammed. A quick glance at the back seat told him the cause of his perilous situation. The sandbag had shifted until it was wedged snugly against the stick. By sheer exertion he managed to inch the stick far enough back so that he could land, but it was a narrow escape. Such experiences, however, did not discourage his great enthusiasm for flying.

During the summer of 1938, the family paid a visit to the United States. They went first to Abilene and then to Denver, returning to the Philippines in the fall. That autumn Eisenhower and his son had many long, informal talks concerning the challenge of events in Europe. September brought the Munich crisis when the British Prime Minister, Neville Chamberlain, went to Germany to meet with Hitler. At a conference with the French premier it was agreed that Germany could annex part of Czechoslovakia. Returning in triumph to announce to a hushed Parliament that there would be "peace in our time," Chamberlain quickly came under severe criticism for the so-called appeasement policy. John Eisenhower was much disturbed by this action. But his father took great pains to explain that he thought Chamberlain was buying time, with always the chance that war might be entirely avoided. Then he drew again a vivid picture of the ultimate horrors of war. He wanted his son to understand the total miseries that war brings, miseries that press upon nations for generations to come and interfere with human progress.

Meanwhile the situation in the Philippines was becoming graver by the hour. The Japanese were already deep into China. There could no longer be any doubt that one of the grand designs of Japanese strategy was the eventual encirclement of the Philippines.

MacArthur and his staff, with Major Eisenhower playing an important role, carefully worked out detailed plans for defending the islands against Japanese attack.

On September 1, 1939, Hitler's army invaded Poland. The global war that Fox Conner had predicted so many years earlier had come at last. Eisenhower felt that he must take leave of the Philippines and return to Washington. It was an agonizing decision, not only because he loved the Filipinos but also because he was under strong pressure to stay. But he wanted to be at the nerve center of the Allied effort. With great sadness, Ike, Mamie and John sailed for America on December 13, 1939.

"Well, Boys, It's Come"

Back home, Ike bounced through a succession of assignments. His first was at Fort Ord, California, where they called him "alarmist Ike" because of his repeated warnings about an approaching war. Nevertheless, he became extremely well liked and respected by his men. In March of 1940 he went to Fort Lewis, Washington. He was now executive officer of the 15th Infantry Division.

That summer his son, John, was faced with the decision of whether to take up a career in the law or in the army. His Uncle Edgar wanted him to study law and then come into his Tacoma law firm. John decided upon the army. He pleased his father immensely by beating the Kansas record (including his dad's) on the West Point entrance examinations.

In November of 1940 Eisenhower became chief of staff of the Third Division, with headquarters still at Fort Lewis. Good staff officers are hard to find, and he was proving to be one of the best. Then in March, 1941, he was appointed chief of staff for the Ninth Army Corps and—even more important—promoted to the rank of full colonel (temporary).

Late that summer an elaborate series of mock battles and maneuvers deep in the steaming southlands of Louisiana played a big role in advancing the already booming career of Colonel Eisenhower. Ike, now chief of staff of the Third Army under General Walter Krueger, did a superb job of conceiving and directing strategy for Krueger's "Blues" in their attack against General Ben Lear's Second Army (the "Reds").

The Blues won, though the decision seemed in doubt for a time because of the irrepressible General Patton, in command of the "Reds'" Second Armored Division. Unaccountably and "impossibly" Patton had wheeled his forces around the Blues' flank and he claimed the victory. But the umpires quickly discovered that during the night Patton had reached his incredible position by illegal means. He had accomplished the "impossible" by digging into his own pockets to buy extra gasoline at service stations to feed his thirsty tanks.

A few days later Eisenhower was promoted to brigadier general. He had worked hard, and the results of

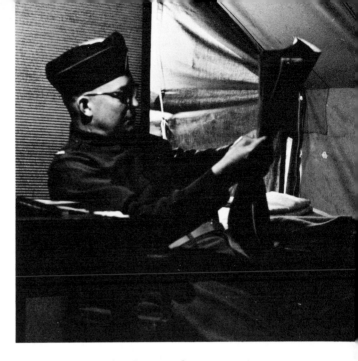

Colonel Eisenhower photographed in his tent during maneuvers.

his careful planning had proved highly successful.

In less than three months, the mock battles staged in August and September had turned out to be rehearsals for the real thing.

On December 7, 1941, Eisenhower was feeling overworked and badly in need of a catnap. He said, "I'm dead beat. I'm going to treat myself to a nap. Call me if anything happens." An hour later the phone rang, waking him from a deep sleep. The Japanese had attacked Pearl Harbor. When he arrived at his office he said simply: "Well, boys, it's come."

A week later Eisenhower arrived in Washington, D.C., where he was to serve under General Leonard Gerow as assistant chief of the War Plans Division. In the nation's capital his fortunes soared. His experience in the Philippines made him invaluable in planning strategy for the Pacific Theater of War. And Eisenhower's relations with General George Marshall, Chief of Staff of the Army, ripened in warmth and depth day by day. The two men hit it off at once. Both were frank, unpretentious and extremely competent, as well as hard workers and great leaders of men. It seemed inevitable that Marshall would have Eisenhower marked for higher stations.

On March 27th the soldier from Abilene was made a major general (temporary), and on April 2nd he was appointed assistant chief of staff in charge of the new Operations Division. The details of responsibility thrust upon him were becoming so burdensome that he was compelled to conserve his time on all fronts. At first he himself dictated a resumé of all conversations or conferences held in connection with war plans. But when this practice proved entirely too time-consuming, he abandoned it in favor of an automatic recording system. The General warned all visitors that his office was completely wired, explaining that this was the only way he could keep a quick, accurate record of all conversations.

Late in May of 1942, General Marshall sent Eisenhower to England to talk to American officers on duty there. He was to bring back recommendations for the future organization and development of United States forces in Europe for their part in the eventual invasion of the Continent. Upon his return, Eisenhower submitted to the Chief of Staff a draft of a "Directive for the Commanding General, European Theater of Operations." It provided for a unified command of all American forces allocated to the European area.

As General Eisenhower himself relates this episode:

> I submitted to the Chief of Staff a draft of a "Directive for the Commanding General, European Theater of Operations," which provided for unified command of all American forces allocated to the European area. I remarked to General Marshall that this was one paper he should read in detail before it went out because it was likely to be an important document in the further waging of the war. His reply still lives in my memory: "I certainly do want to read it. You may be the man who executes it. If that's the case, when can you leave?" Three days later General Marshall told me definitely that I would command the European theater.

At last Eisenhower was to be sprung from his desk and thrust into the field in an exhilarating command post. There followed a round of conferences with important men, including President Franklin D. Roosevelt and Winston Churchill, the British Prime Minister, who paid a visit to the United States during June, 1942. It was Churchill's first private meeting with Eisenhower and he later wrote: "We had a most agreeable discussion lasting over an hour. . . . Thus began a friendship which across all the ups and downs of war I have preserved with deep satisfaction . . ."

John Eisenhower came to Washington from West
Point for a brief visit with his parents. Then on June 22nd,
Ike left for London. He had chosen a naval lieutenant
commander, Harry C. Butcher, as his assistant. Selecting
a naval officer for such an assignment was most unusual.
But Eisenhower had a ready explanation for this choice
of an old friend. "I have to have someone with me
who is not subservient," he said. "Someone I can trust."

General Mark Clark and several other assistants
accompanied Eisenhower when he left Washington
to assume command of the European Theater of
Operations, United States Army. Headquarters had been
set up in the heart of London in Grosvenor Square,
with its serene, aristocratic Georgian-style houses. With
his usual punch and practicality, Eisenhower started
organizational plans swinging ahead on all levels. He
put together a close-knit staff which, by fall, included
the invaluable Brigadier General Walter Bedell Smith,
as Eisenhower's chief of staff. Relations with their
British counterparts got off to a good start and soon the
Services of Supply began the monumental task of setting
up ports, airfields, camps, and warehouses to accom-
modate men and equipment. At first the shipments
were barely a trickle, but before many months they
began to flood the British Isles. They turned a country
slightly smaller than the State of Wyoming into a super-
arsenal for the Allied countries.

In England it was not just the billeting and training
of men that concerned Ike. He was deeply concerned

with their education and morale as well. Two thoughts he particularly wanted to impress upon his troops. First, they must be aware of the sacrifices and courage of the British people, who had stood virtually alone for more than a year against the Nazis. These courageous people would certainly become unhappy with American soldiers who regarded the war as a European quarrel and smugly felt their participation in it was a gift rather than a duty in a hostile world. Second, he wanted to make doubly sure that his troops understood clearly not

General Eisenhower autographs a drum at the opening of an American Red Cross Club in London (July 4, 1942).

only that they had to fight, but *why* they had to fight. He knew that to fight well, they had to fight from conviction.

Quite apart from promoting mutual understanding, it was urgent that the Allies begin at once to plan strategy meetings for the invasion of Europe. The preparation time required for the invasion was obviously going to be considerably longer than anyone had anticipated. Initially the Allies had hoped to make a landing in France by the following spring of 1943. But a careful calculation of power showed that the build-up would take much longer. Any cross-Channel invasion during the fall months of 1943 would be dangerous. So the Allies were faced with the disappointing decision of postponing a major offensive until the spring of 1944.

No hint of the time required for preparations could be revealed. To do so would give the Germans too clear a picture of how little prepared the Allies really were. It would also have a discouraging effect upon public opinion, which was already at low ebb from staggering setbacks for the British in the Egyptian desert, Japanese triumphs in the Pacific and the grim hardships on the Russian front, where the Germans and Russians were engaged in a life-or-death struggle. Nothing must be allowed to endanger the spirit of Allied coöperation. If they did not pull together, they could never hope to win.

After considering what smaller campaigns might be undertaken in the Middle East, Northwest Africa, or perhaps even France, the United States and Britain reached a decision on July 24, 1942, to proceed with the invasion of Northwest Africa. General Eisenhower was appointed Allied commander in chief of the expedition, and the very first offensive action—named TORCH— went into hurried preparation.

There were many "firsts" in this campaign. Never before had any nation attempted a major invasion of another land from such a distance. Many of the troops and supplies came 3,500 miles from the United States. Also, TORCH was to be the first major Allied amphibious landing of the war. It would teach valuable lessons for the eventual cross-Channel invasion of Europe. Finally, TORCH was the first real joint Allied invasion effort. It was to prove that such coöperation really could work. Eisenhower has often pointed out that one reason for Napoleon's success is the fact that he always managed to take on his antagonists one at a time. On the one occasion when his enemies joined to oppose him in battle, he met his Waterloo.

That the alliance functioned so smoothly was to be one of General Eisenhower's most subtle and far-reaching contributions to his job as commander in chief, both in the major European invasion, and in North Africa. He later wrote:

> . . . personal characteristics are more important than ever before in warfare. . . . the teams and staffs through which the modern commander absorbs information and exercises his authority must be a beautifully interlocked, smooth-working mechanism. . . . The high commander must therefore be calm, clear, and deter-

mined—and in all commands, especially allied organizations, his success will be measured more by his ability to lead and persuade than by his adherence to fixed notions of arbitrary command practices.

Another problem just as thorny as the joint business of planning the strategy, tactics and organization to put the campaign into effect, was the delicate political situation in Northwest Africa. The government the Allies were going to attack in North Africa was a *French* government—part of the supposedly neutral Vichy regime in unoccupied southern France. The French had sued for peace after their disastrous defeats when the Germans invaded their country. And a puppet French government, collaborating with the Germans, had been set up at Vichy. While some French troops, including General Charles de Gaulle, had escaped to England, others had remained loyal to the legal French government. The British therefore felt they had been abandoned to fight alone. They were particularly upset that the French fleet, instead of fighting side by side with the British Royal Navy to overcome the menace of the deadly U-boat, was not only out of the scrap but, worse, in danger of falling into German hands.

The supreme mission of the Allies prior to the invasion was to persuade the North African French to come over willingly to the Allied side. Or at the very least they should be urged to offer only token resistance to the invasion. If, instead, the French resisted strongly, everyone agreed that the invasion had little chance of succeeding. It would be blasted back into the sea.

Since it was assumed that the French, in their pride, might be more antagonistic to the British than the Americans, it was planned that most of the assault troops would be American. The British troops would be held back as reinforcements.

For four months the days were filled with thousands of messages, queries, orders, and conferences. It was a time of urgent training, allocation and reallocation of scarce equipment, saddening losses to the German U-boats, and unceasing attention to every detail of the complicated TORCH master plan. Finally, on November 5th, General Eisenhower moved his headquarters to the British fortress of Gibraltar, which guards the entrance to the Mediterranean. Here, deep in the underground passages, he and his staff planned and waited impatiently while the armadas carrying arms and men and the hopes of millions steamed toward the landing points at Casablanca, Oran and Algiers.

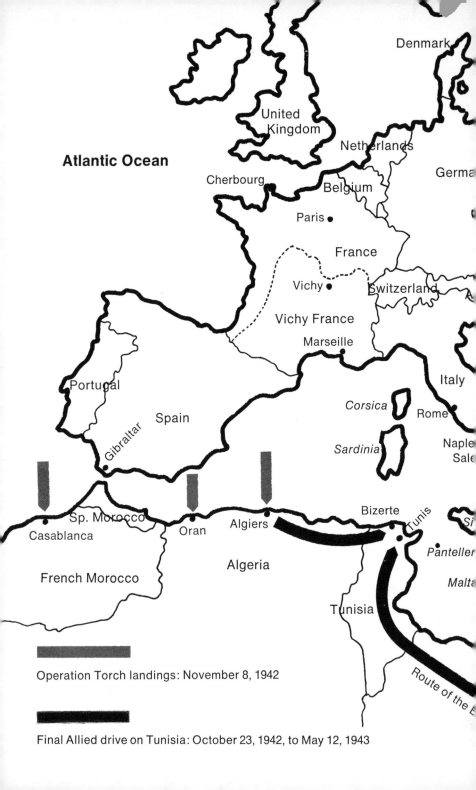

Operation Torch landings: November 8, 1942

Final Allied drive on Tunisia: October 23, 1942, to May 12, 1943

Decisive Allied Campaigns in North Africa

Poland

U.S.S.R.

oslovakia

gary

Rumania

oslavia

Bulgaria

Black Sea

Albania

Greece

Turkey

Crete

Cyprus

Mediterranean Sea

El Alamein

Suez Canal

ghth Army

Cairo

Egypt

Libya

Tri-Target Triumph

The tensest days of the war for Eisenhower, he later remarked, were November 7th and 8th of 1942. Stormy seas threatened to halt the Casablanca assault. Any postponement might result in near catastrophe, for all the advantages of surprise would be lost. German planes and U-boats would take a heavy toll of the directionless ships; the French in North Africa might stiffen into defiance, and the Germans might even persuade Spain to end her neutrality.

But at the last moment there was a break in the weather, and operation TORCH proceeded as scheduled. Spilling out of a vast fleet of warships and transport and cargo ships, men and materiel streamed into Africa. Fortunately prior intelligence work among French officers in Algiers resulted in little opposition on that front. But at Oran the Allied assault forces met bitter resistance, which was not overcome for several days. Communication with Casablanca broke down, to Eisenhower's great concern, and all he knew was that at some points the fight was raging hot.

For TORCH to succeed, Eisenhower had to excel not only as a military strategist but as an astute statesman as well. At great risk, French General Henri Giraud

With a group of British and American officers at his Gibraltar headquarters, Ike makes a final checkup on French Moroccan invasion plans.

had been secretly transported from France to Gibraltar. The Allies hoped he would be willing and able to lead the French of North Africa to their support. After an initial disappointment that his role was not to be the commanding one, Giraud agreed to try to rally the loyalty of the North Africans. The Allies, gambling on his success, flew him to Algiers with General Mark Clark on November 9th. There he broadcast. directly to the people. But it soon became obvious that he could command no support.

In the meantime Eisenhower had learned that Admiral Jean Darlan, supreme commander of the French fleet, was in Algiers visiting his sick son. Here was a fresh opportunity. General Eisenhower knew that there would be loud outcries in both England and the United States if he bargained with such a pro-German supporter of the Vichy government instead of clapping him into jail. But the American commander had to consider the broader strategy and not bow to emotionalism. He felt sure that the French forces would obey only Darlan, as commander in chief of French forces in North Africa, and that there would be bloody fighting if the invading forces could not make an ally of him.

General Clark acted for Eisenhower in the delicate negotiations. On November 10th Darlan finally ordered the French to stop fighting. Old Marshal Pétain, head of the Vichy government, furiously countermanded this cease-fire and ordered Darlan dismissed. But General Clark refused to let Darlan recall his order. Then when Darlan learned that Germany had just violated the 1940

French-German Armistice by occupying southern France, he offered his complete coöperation. In return, Eisenhower agreed to British and American approval for Darlan to assume authority as head of the local French government in North Africa. General Giraud was to become commander of military forces in Northwest Africa.

November 13th brought the end of the first phase of operations in Northwest Africa.

Although there was considerable criticism of Eisenhower's decision in the British and American newspapers, he felt he had made the most practical choice. As he himself explained in a telegram to Roosevelt and Churchill:

> Our hope of quick conquest of Tunisia and of gaining here a supporting population cannot be realized unless there is accepted a general agreement along the lines which we have just made with Darlan and the other officials who control the administrative machinery of the region . . . Without a strong French government we would be forced to undertake military occupation. The cost in time and resources would be tremendous. In Morocco alone General Patton believes that it would require 60,000 Allied troops . . .

Churchill replied: "Anything for the battle, but the politics will have to be sorted out later on."

On November 23rd General Eisenhower moved from Gibraltar to Algiers. He set up his headquarters in the St. George Hotel, which stood on a hill overlooking the city. He soon christened his office "Grand

Admiral Jean Darlan with General Eisenhower.

Central Station," because so many people were constantly running in and out.

He had wanted to be closer to the action, but all fighting soon ceased in the west. Morocco and Algeria belonged to the Allies, and French West Africa with the important base of Dakar was brought into the fold by its governor, Pierre Boisson. Full attention could now be paid to Tunisia and points farther east.

Egypt had become a brighter patch on Africa's eastern front. In late October General Sir Bernard L. Montgomery had led his seasoned Eighth Army into battle against the brilliant German commander, General

Erwin Rommel. The result was one of the great Allied victories of the war at El Alamein. Montgomery's men forced the Germans and their Italian allies out of Egypt back west into Libya. Now Eisenhower wanted to squeeze the Germans from the other side, by the speedy capture of northern Tunisia. Allied control of the ports of Tunis and Bizerte would cut the Axis lines of communication and strangle the flow of supplies from Sicily to the Axis armies in Tunisia and Libya.

The British First Army was assigned to this task. To succeed, speed and boldness were of prime importance, for the Germans were pouring troops into Tunisia. The British commander, General Sir Kenneth Anderson, was handicapped by lack of transportation equipment, unseasonably rainy weather, and an army that was significantly under strength. Eisenhower tried to bolster his forces, and December 24th was set for the final, all-out attack. But in the end the venture proved impossible. As the General himself later wrote:

> I was determined not to give up unless personally convinced that the attack was an impossibility. Weather prohibited flying and I started forward by automobile on December 22, encountering miserable road conditions from the moment we left Algiers. Traveling almost incessantly, I met General Anderson at his headquarters in the early morning of December 24 and with him proceeded at once to . . . the headquarters of the British 5 Corps, which was to make the attack . . .
>
> The rain fell constantly. We went out personally to inspect the countryside over which the troops would

have to advance, and while doing so I observed an incident which, as much as anything else, I think, convinced me of the hopelessness of an attack. About thirty feet off the road, in a field that appeared to be covered with winter wheat, a motorcycle had become stuck in the mud. Four soldiers were struggling to extricate it but in spite of their most strenuous efforts succeeded only in getting themselves mired into the sticky clay. They finally had to give up the attempt and left the motorcycle more deeply bogged down than when they started.

We went back to headquarters and I directed that the attack be indefinitely postponed. It was a bitter decision. . . .

In such circumstances it is always necessary for the commander to avoid an attitude of defeatism; discouragement on the part of the high commander inevitably spreads rapidly throughout the command and always with unfortunate results. On that occasion it was exceedingly difficult to display any particular optimism.

The line was extended south by brave but sparse and ill-armed French garrisons, along with some American troops. But all they could do was to preserve their defensive position during the next few months.

Meantime the political situation in Northwest Africa was proving as unsettled as the military one farther east. Darlan was assassinated on December 24th and General Giraud succeeded him. But General Giraud showed little interest in administration. All he wanted was to build up his troops. Yet the civil government was far too shaky and disorganized to be neglected. The Vichyites, Free French, Arabs and Jews were scrapping among themselves. Added to that, the economy was near rock-bottom. General Charles de Gaulle, leader of the Free French in London, was eager to get to Africa and take control, but the Allies were still against such a move.

One bright streak in this trying period for Eisenhower was a visit with his brother Milton, who had been sent to Algiers by the Office of War Information. From Milton, Ike learned for the first time just how ill-informed public opinion was in the States, and how much criticized he was for the way he was dealing with North African political and economic problems. As a result he made various changes in the handling of military censorship and civilian-controlled psychological warfare.

On January 14, 1943, Churchill and Roosevelt met for an historic ten-day conference at Casablanca. In many ways the timing of this meeting marked the turning point of the war. On the Eastern Front, Russia was beginning to rout the Germans along their over-extended lines during a winter offensive. Stalingrad, which the Russians had defended with legendary bravery, was soon to be dramatically rescued, and battered Leningrad relieved from a seventeen-month seige. In the Pacific the Japanese thrust had passed its height. During May of 1942 the United States Navy had kept the Japanese from Australia in the Battle of the Coral Sea; in June it successfully defended Midway Island from attack. That August the United States Marines landed in the Solomon Islands and began the

Generals Giraud (left) and de Gaulle agree to shake hands at the Casablanca conference. President Roosevelt and Prime Minister Churchill (right) watch.

long fight for Guadalcanal.

At the Casablanca meeting the major strategy of a cross-Channel invasion was reaffirmed and plans were laid for assembling in England the forces for a giant attack. To speed the day, the air offensive against Germany and the campaign against U-boats were to be intensified. Meanwhile the Soviet Union would be given as much equipment as could be spared. And perhaps most immediately significant for Eisenhower, the Combined Chiefs of Staff laid plans to invade Sicily during the summer in a drive to knock Italy out of the war and give the Germans fresh problems on a new front. Eisenhower was to continue in overall command.

The General attended the Casablanca conference for just one day. And his flight there almost proved a disaster, for two of the engines on his plane conked out. The pilot had his passengers standing by the escape hatches with parachutes strapped on during the last fifty miles of the flight. Ike, thinking of his old West Point knee, was not relishing the idea of a jump.

The most difficult personality at the Casablanca Conference was General de Gaulle. He was claiming leadership of the French, and wanted no part of General Giraud. They agreed to shake hands, but accomplished little else at that time.

Also at the conference the Allies set as the ultimate goal of the European war the unconditional surrender of the Axis powers.

Less than a month after the conference, Eisenhower received another promotion. He was made a full general on February 11th. Until this time he had been outranked by many of the officers serving under him.

For the approaching Tunisian campaign Eisenhower's deputy commander was General Sir Harold Alexander. Air Chief Marshall Sir Arthur W. Tedder and Admiral Sir Andrew Browne Cunningham were his air and navy commanders in chief. All three were veteran British fighting men, but to quote the words of Eisenhower himself:

"This development was extraordinarily pleasing to me because it meant, first and foremost, complete unity of action in the central Mediterranean and it provided needed machinery for effective tactical and strategical coordination."

After a somewhat shaky start, the Allied drive to throw the enemy out of North Africa really began to roll on March 20th. By May 12th the Allied forces had achieved their goals. The Axis resistance in North Africa was ended, and the Germans and Italians had been pushed across the Mediterranean. The victory in Africa showed the world that the Allies were on the march at last.

As for the lessons learned by the Allies during the African campaign, Eisenhower was later to write:

Within the African theater one of the greatest products of the victory was the progress achieved in the welding of Allied unity and the establishment of a command team that was already showing the effects of a growing confidence and trust among all its members. . . . Immediate and continuous loyalty to the concept of unity and to allied commanders is basic to victory. The instant such commanders lose the confidence of either government or of the majority of their principal subordinates, they must be relieved.

This was the great Allied lesson of Tunisia. . . .

Italy Leaves the Axis

Long before the final victory in Africa, Eisenhower was deep into plans for the invasion of the rocky island of Sicily. By the middle of May there was still much grueling work ahead. Weeks before the landing, every conceivably necessary item must be secured, and loaded in the proper order in the holds of ships. But this time, Ike knew he had a command team that was welded together into a working unit. Alexander was in command, with Montgomery and Patton leading the infantry. (The latter, Eisenhower's old friend from Camp Meade days, had particularly distinguished himself during the final phases of the fighting in Africa.)

71

General Tedder would again command the air forces, with Cunningham in charge of the navies.

As always, surprise was a key factor in the planning and success of the Sicilian invasion. To keep the Axis guessing, feints were made toward Sardinia and Corsica on the west side of the Mediterranean, and toward Crete on the east. At the same time, Allied bombers were softening up the defenses on Sicily.

Eisenhower took one of his most unorthodox steps at this time. He knew that if the reporters were to continue speculating freely in their papers, they would see just enough to be able to make an intelligent guess about where the Allies were going next. So he let them in on the plans, and asked them to help keep the secret secure. The reporters were stunned, but never have so many kept a secret so well.

As a preliminary step, it was decided to take the small Italian island of Pantelleria which lies between the northeast coast of Tunisia and Sicily. Churchill bet Ike that there were not more than three thousand men defending it, and said he would pay five centimes each (or one-twentieth of a cent) for every Italian soldier over that number. After a six-day period of intensive day and night bombing, the Allied landing force began to disembark on June 11th, only to discover the disheartened Italians surrendering before the invaders set foot to ground. Just one casualty was reported: a soldier bitten by a mule. Ike collected from Churchill—there were eleven thousand prisoners. The captured island, incidentally, provided an invaluable airfield for

After six days and nights of bombing, nothing but rubble remained in the streets of Pantelleria.

use in the invasion of Sicily.

July 8th found Eisenhower in Malta, England's Mediterranean island base. Because the naval communications at Malta were excellent, the Allies had selected it for their headquarters during the opening phases of the Sicilian invasion. The island had been pounded almost to rubble by Axis bombs but remained stubbornly resistant.

John Gunther, the well-known author, was in Malta as a special war correspondent just before the Sicily invasion, and he has written the following interesting account of an interview with Eisenhower:

> I myself first met Eisenhower at a press conference in July, 1943, in Malta, and . . . I was stupefied and amazed at what went on. Here was the commander in chief of one of the most stupendous operations in military history, on the very day before it was to take place; yet he spent sixty-five minutes in solid, earnest, friendly give-and-take with a group of newspapermen and press officers, discussing matters so utterly remote from his own direct responsibilities as radio routes to Tunis and the like. His frankness was exceptional. . . . With zest and a bright eye for news he began to sketch the kind of stories we might write. . . . But he insisted on one rule: nothing about himself personally. No word at all about Eisenhower the man, except when mention of the commander in chief was essential to the story, and then only in connection with his fellow officers of the Allied high command.

On the evening of July 9th, with the wind so high that the invasion was in danger of foundering, Ike stood

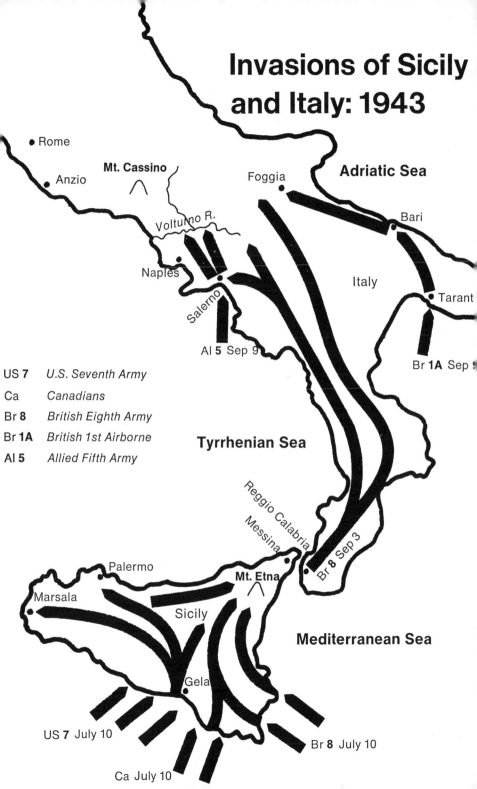

Invasions of Sicily and Italy: 1943

Rome

Anzio

Mt. Cassino

Foggia

Adriatic Sea

Bari

Voltumo R.

Naples

Italy

Salerno

Tarant

Al **5** Sep 9

Br **1A** Sep

US **7**   *U.S. Seventh Army*

Ca   *Canadians*

Br **8**   *British Eighth Army*

Br **1A**   *British 1st Airborne*

Al **5**   *Allied Fifth Army*

Tyrrhenian Sea

Reggio Calabria

Messina

Br **8** Sep 3

Palermo

Mt. Etna

Marsala

Sicily

Mediterranean Sea

Gela

US **7** July 10

Br **8** July 10

Ca July 10

on a hill, nervously fingering his lucky coins (an American silver dollar, a British gold piece and a French franc). As he put it, "There was nothing we could do but pray." It was too late for postponement. The invasion ships had already sailed from North Africa.

That night the first British and American paratroops leaped from their plane hatches onto the rocky island. Many were blown far from their targets, but they rallied superbly. Then at early dawn on July 10th, the first sea-borne units landed, and LSTs (Landing Ship, Tank) spewed forth their men, tanks, trucks, and guns. The invading forces were split into three groups with the Americans to the west, the Canadians in the center, and the British to the east.

The Italians, badly armed, hungry and lacking any heart for a fight, gave up fairly soon. But Montgomery's British troops, driving northward to Messina, soon came up against strong German units, dug into the side of Sicily's majestic volcano, Mt. Etna. Here the British General and his men settled down to sound out the German positions, while Patton's American forces swept around the west side of Sicily, sometimes pelted with flowers and almonds rather than bullets. They captured Marsala and Palermo. German resistance became stiffer along the north coast, where the terrain was discouragingly well suited for defensive fighting. The Americans had to fight their way across a succession of ridges and valleys, while the Germans retreated from one high point to another, dominating the scrubby, dusty land through which American infantry had to crawl. Patton conserved as many men as he could, using air power to blast not only the German positions but their supply and communication lines. Meanwhile the Navy stood off from the shore firing its great guns up the narrow defiles. Several times landing parties were sent forward by sea to outflank the Germans and force a withdrawal.

Despite stubborn German resistance, August 18th found victorious Allied troops astride the rubble of Messina, port of departure for the escaping Fascist soldiers. After thirty-eight days of fierce fighting Sicily had been taken.

An Allied reconnaissance unit searches for enemy snipers in one of the battered streets of Messina, Sicily.

The final outcome, however, came as no surprise to Eisenhower. Two days after the Sicily landings he had another talk with the press. And again, in the words of Mr. Gunther:

> He was working in a damp cubicle not bigger than ten feet by fourteen; there was a single table covered by a gray blanket and a white blotter; an oil heater was burning, but the clay floor was wet and cold. The General . . . seemed very pleased at the way the campaign was going. "By golly," he kept muttering, "I don't understand it! By golly, I think we've done it again!" By this he meant that the amphibious operations had taken the enemy completely unawares, and that there had been no serious attack on our landing craft though they were sitting ducks. The General rocked back on his wicker chair, his heels caught in the lower rung. He grinned from cheek to cheek . . .

On the eighteenth of July, Eisenhower cabled to the Combined Chiefs of Staff his recommendation that as soon as they had taken Messina they should follow up their victory by crossing the strait and carrying the war to the Italian mainland. By this time the significance of the attack from the south was becoming obvious to all.

Massive unrest was now churning the Italian political scene. On July 25th Italy's Fascist leader, Benito Mussolini, had been overthrown and imprisoned. He was later rescued by German paratroopers in a daring escape plan and set up as a puppet dictator in the north of Italy. But Marshal Badoglio took over as the head of the legal Italian government. For a time he wavered over whether to capitulate or fight, but finally on September 3, 1943—the day that British and American troops crossed the Straits of Messina onto the tip of the Italian boot—a secret armistice was signed. On the 8th the Italians surrendered unconditionally.

The first Axis nation had been thrown to the mat. But Germany continued to give stubborn defensive resistance under Albert von Kesselring. Much bloody fighting on Italian soil was yet to come. The terrain was tough, marked by mountains and rivers, most favorable to those fighting on the defensive. The Germans fought for every foot of ground and when they retreated they did their best to leave the countryside in ruins. They blew up bridges and blasted down cut-ins on mountain roads. The Allied forces had to carry out repairs under heavy fire, and the engineers suffered many casualties.

One of the grimmest Allied scars of the Italian campaign was inflicted at Salerno on September 9th. General Mark Clark commanded a costly Allied Fifth Army landing at this site near Naples, while on the other side of the Italian boot the Eighth Army under Montgomery took Taranto and Bari, and headed for the airfields of Foggia. Past the watchtowers, castles and temples of ancient Italy, the flood of war crept up the Italian peninsula. It was a painfully slow struggle against tough German resistance, mountains, floods and winter cold. By early November the Allies were about seventy-five miles south of Rome, but they could not penetrate the German lines. "All roads lead to Rome,"

During a tour of the Italian front, the Commanding General stops to chat with an enlisted man.

In the "war room" of the 3rd Division (Italy), Eisenhower and General Mark Clark (third from left) confer with two fellow officers.

said General Alexander, "but unfortunately all of them are mined."

General Eisenhower had been in the Mediterranean for just a year now, but he was soon to depart. For some time there had been rumors about a possible change for Ike. The most persistent was that General George Marshall would be placed in command of the forthcoming cross-Channel invasion of Europe from England, and Eisenhower would be sent to Washington to replace him as Chief of Staff. Then in early December of 1943, Eisenhower met President Roosevelt at Tunis after the President's return from the top-level Allied conferences at Cairo and Tehran. The General later reported the events of this historic meeting as follows:

> The President arrived in midafternoon and was scarcely seated in the automobile when he cleared up the matter with one short sentence. He said, "Well, Ike, you are going to command Overlord."

Eisenhower was to be supreme commander of the cross-Channel invasion of Europe, with his headquarters in London. Alexander would take over his command in the Mediterranean theater.

On Christmas day, 1943, Ike visited his troops on the Italian front for the last time. Although reluctant to give up a command in which he was so completely immersed, he could be grateful for the big change in Allied fortunes. Africa and the Middle East were now safe from attack or subversion. Slow progress was being made in the Pacific. And Russia was gathering momentum in her drive for East Prussia.

For a brief, warming interlude General Eisenhower rejoined his family in America. Mrs. Eisenhower was in Washington, and she and her husband boarded General Marshall's private railway car in secret. Some hours later the car was detached on a siding, hidden from view, below the granite wall of West Point. It was an intense pleasure to Ike to see his cadet son again and have one of those free-wheeling talks they had so enjoyed when John was a boy. Part of their time together they spent in arguing about whether John should go into the Infantry or the Artillery.

After this happy reunion, the General flew to Kansas for a visit with his mother and brothers Arthur and Milton. For security reasons he could not go to Abilene; instead the family gathered at Manhattan, Kansas. Then he returned east, and on January 12th boarded the plane that would take him back to London—and the war.

The Lion and the Eagle – D-Day

By mid-January of 1944 Ike was headquartered' in the Bushey Park area just outside London. Here, surrounded by many experienced and dedicated aides, he plunged into the flurry of preparation and plans for "Operation Overlord," as the European invasion project was called. Air Chief Marshal Tedder was his deputy; "Beedle" Smith continued as his indispensable chief of staff. Admiral Sir Bertram Ramsay was commander of the combined naval forces, and Air Chief Marshal Sir Trafford Leigh-Mallory commanded the combined air forces. Montgomery was put in charge of all army forces for the opening phases of the European invasion.

Afterward the British and American forces would split, with General Omar Bradley as American Army Group Commander.

SHAEF (Supreme Headquarters, Allied Expeditionary Forces) soon buzzed with activity. A large planning staff had already been working many months on preliminary plans under Britain's Lieutenant General Frederick Morgan. These initial plans called for landing forces of three divisions backed up by two follow-up divisions. Eisenhower wanted five divisions with two

A group of "Operation Overlord" leaders meet in London. Sitting, left to right: Air Chief Marshal Sir Arthur Tedder, General Eisenhower, General Sir Bernard Montgomery. Standing, left to right: General Omar Bradley, Admiral Sir Bertram Ramsay, Air Chief Marshal Sir Trafford Leigh-Mallory, General Walter Bedell Smith.

follow-up divisions afloat. These would be the beachhead forces, to be followed by division after division once the first breakthrough had been achieved. The Allies expected to have sixty-eight divisions on the continent by the time they crossed the Rhine River into the German heartland.

The scope of the Allied effort and the complexity of the planning that went into launching the invasion of the Continent is staggering to contemplate. In the first hundred days following D-Day alone, 2,200,000 men, 450,000 vehicles and 4,000,000 tons of supplies were landed on the shell-pocked shores of Normandy.

While preparing for Overlord the Allies struck with air blows where they could hurt the most. The purpose was clear: to destroy German forces and resources. The first goal of the air force was to defeat the German Luftwaffe. German airstrips and airplane factories became prime bombing targets in a successful campaign to gain complete and continuing mastery of the air. The second goal was to cripple German forces on the ground, particularly by destroying the source of their supplies and their supply routes. Royal Air Force units flew by night, while American precision bombers dropped their lethal loads of TNT by day. Bigger and faster came the raids. "The time will come," Eisenhower told his pilots in April, "when you will be flying from dawn to dusk."

Once fixed, the grand invasion strategy for defeating the German forces on the continent itself never changed in its essentials. Eisenhower insisted that the overall plan remain constant, while tactics—maneuvering in the field—must always be flexible. Germany's defense, if she could be pushed back out of France and Belgium, would be to fall back on her dug-in Siegfried Line on the border between those two countries and the German homeland. Behind this line—beyond the majestic, slow-moving waters of the river Rhine—was her second line of defense.

Allied strategy, after landing and breakout, called for heading west with three armies. The two northerly forces would strike across northern France and Belgium, liberating Paris and freeing Belgium's excellent ports for Allied use. Then they would push on through the lower Netherlands, entering Germany and coming up to the Rhine River across from and north of the most important industrial section of Germany, the Ruhr Valley.

The third army would attack farther down. It would pierce the lower half of the Siegfried Line, which defended the Saar, Germany's second most important industrial district. These forces would then link up with Allied troops invading the southern coast of France from the Mediterranean. In this way the Allied line would be extended almost the full length of the Rhine River.

By such strategy, the Allies planned to defeat the flower of the German forces on the west side of the Rhine while the Allied supply line was short and the German supply line long. The way would then be clear for an attack all along the Rhine, with the major push coming in the north to encircle the Ruhr. A secondary push would encircle the Ruhr from the south. This is a maneuver known as a "double envelopment" in military terminology. Once it was accomplished, Germany would crumple; she would be beaten to her knees.

As soon as the general plan was set, Eisenhower and the Overlord Operation Staff confined their attention to the details of the D-Day invasion and the battle of France—beachhead and breakout. For the landings, they chose five beaches along a sixty-mile segment of the crescent of the Normandy coast, from the Orne River west to beyond the Vire River. Three British and Canadian groups were to land on the Orne River side at beaches with the code names of Sword, Juno and Gold. Farther west, or to the right, the Americans were to land at sectors called Omaha Beach and Utah Beach.

The sharpest disagreement was over the landing at Utah Beach. Several planners advised against it because they feared the strip would be difficult to hold, backed up as it is by a wide lagoon. They worried that the Germans would hold the causeways and bottle up the forces. Two fine divisions might be slaughtered. Eisenhower, however, wanted one landing actually out on the Cherbourg peninsula. Without it, he thought, all the forces might be in danger of being boxed in. Also the Allies could make good use of the Cherbourg port if they captured it. Acting on this belief, he decided to go ahead with the Utah landing. He would back up the assault waves by dropping parachutists and gliders behind the lagoon.

It was an agonizing decision to have to make, and it had to be made twice because Sir Marshal Leigh-Mallory brought up the question a second time just a few days before D-Day. He advised Eisenhower that he should anticipate a terrible disaster, with a loss of seventy percent of the glider troops and fifty percent of the paratroops. Eisenhower later described most vividly the difficulty of reaching a decision on the problem:

> I went to my tent alone and sat down to think. Over and over I reviewed each step . . . I realized, of course, that if I deliberately disregarded the advice of my technical expert on the subject, and his predictions should prove accurate, then I would carry to my grave the unbearable burden of a conscience justly accusing me of the stupid, blind sacrifice of thousands of the flower of our youth. Outweighing any personal burden, however, was the possibility that if he were right the effect of the disaster would be far more than local: it would be likely to spread to the entire force.

In the end he decided that the attack would proceed as planned.

There were other hard decisions. How would the French react to the bombing of German troops and supply lines? Such bombings would also imperil French lives and property. Churchill feared the worst. But Eisenhower insisted that German supply lines and communications must be disrupted from the air. Allied troops must receive all the support humanly possible.

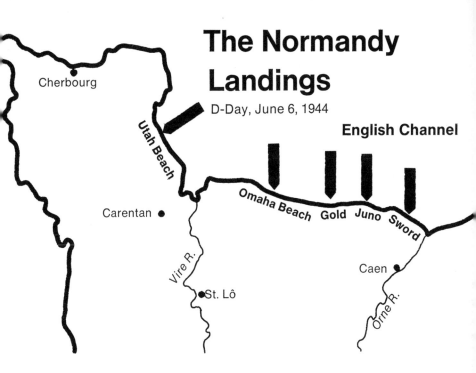

The Normandy Landings

D-Day, June 6, 1944

English Channel

Cherbourg

Utah Beach

Carentan

Omaha Beach Gold Juno Sword

Vire R.

St. Lô

Caen

Orne R.

It was agonizing, too, to have to postpone the invasion from May to June. There were only a few days each month which would bring the right combination of moon, tide and sunrise. The earlier the attack could be launched the better. An early start would allow time for a longer campaign before winter. The Germans would have less time to strengthen their coastal defenses and develop threatening new weapons.

Finally, everything was set for the triphibian invasion. The Germans, of course, knew of the preparations. But they had no idea exactly where or when the Allied armada would be launched. Some of their generals were convinced that the invading force would steer for the Calais area, because the run from Dover, England, to Calais is the shortest distance across the Channel. The Allies helped to foster this delusion. With masterful fakery, the British assembled a phantom "First Army Group" at Dover. Nevertheless Field Marshal Rommel, one of the German anti-invasion commanders, continued to reinforce his Normandy defenses, for he thought the Allies might land there.

Eisenhower, meanwhile, had moved his headquarters in secrecy to Portsmouth. There he worked on the final plans and waited with his advisers for the weather forecasts of his meteorological section. The invasion forces must go forward on June 4th, 5th or 6th if they were to move at all in June. At this crucial point, the essential loneliness of the man at the focal point of responsibility became clear. Dwight D. Eisenhower— and no other—would have to make the final decision to attack, and send the Allied armies to the testing ground of France.

Twice each day—at 4:00 A.M. and at 9:30 P.M.— a small, serious group of men gathered to hear the weather projections. The news was uniformly disturbing: bad weather ahead. June 4th rolled round. At the 4:00 A.M. meeting the commanders had to decide whether or not it would be feasible to move the next day. Some troops were already at sea with replacements pouring in to fill their camps. When Eisenhower asked his commanders in chief whether they were willing to launch their forces, the answers came: Admiral Ramsay —neutral; Air Marshal Tedder—no; General Montgomery—go. Eisenhower's final decision was to hold. A second time of decision came in the early hours of June 5th as the taut-faced group assembled once again. The rain-drenched winds still howled. But this time, miraculously, the meteorologists had something positive to offer. By the next morning the storms would lift, and the weather would be moderately fair for approximately thirty-six hours. This period, however, would be followed by more bad storms. Could enough troops and supplies be landed during the short period of calm? Would they be able to launch the paratroop division?

By 4:15 A.M. the die was cast. General Eisenhower had made the momentous decision. June 6, 1944, would be one of history's landmarks.

Meantime, the Supreme Commander had to live through some of the longest hours of his life. With the gears of war set in motion, little more could be done until reports began to come in after the landings. For weeks, he had been visiting troops to stiffen morale. On this most significant evening he paid a last visit to one of his units—the U.S. 101st Airborne. It was the mission of this division to drop behind Utah Beach. Their spirits were high as they nerved themselves for one of the most gallant episodes of the war. At midnight the last troop plane trundled into the air, and Ike went back to camp to wait for time to pass judgment on his decision.

At last reports began to come in. The American airborne landings behind Utah Beach and the battle of Utah Beach itself seemed to be going encouragingly

The Supreme Commander talks to men of the 101st Airborne on the eve of D-Day.

well. The same was also true of the landing on the
left flank by the British units. The forces at Omaha
Beach, however, were encountering extremely heavy
opposition. Actually, the Allies had expected the fighting
to be as fierce throughout the landing area as it was
at Omaha Beach.

The next day Eisenhower paid a visit to the front,
talking with Montgomery and Bradley, his two commanders in the field. At Omaha Beach he saw the
wrecked landing boats on the shore, the wounded and
the newly dead, the fear and elation. He talked to as
many men as he could, showing a concern for their
individual views and hardships that reflected his belief
in the value of the individual. During this period his
life became a series of trips to the front, visits to troops
about to embark from England, conferences on strategy
and tactics, and meetings on supply.

The fighting grew fiercer as Rommel rushed up what
troops he could muster from the Brittany Peninsula, the
south of France and the Low Countries. The most
powerful contests developed to the east, on the left end
of the line, where the British 2nd Army and Canadian
1st were battling. The Germans still had their largest
body of reserves in the more northerly Calais area.
Should the British succeed in their drive toward Caen,
they would divide the German forces—a disaster Rommel wanted to avoid at all costs.

On the right, American forces battled past the
marshes to the hedgerows, measuring their gains almost
in feet. The hedgerows divided the countryside into

GIs advance through a breach made in a hedgerow.

tiny plots, and were made of a thick heap of dirt with a thorny thicket on top. They interfered with long-range Allied observation, and gave magnificent cover and camouflage to the Germans, who could sit tight and pick off the advancing enemy. Tanks trying to penetrate the hedgerows would climb almost vertically, exposing their vulnerable underbellies to sharp-shooting German guns.

Most of the time the weather was not kind. June

19th set a forty-year record for storms, with a hurricane that stopped all landing activity, grounded the planes, and made life miserable for the infantry.

Fierce fighting went on and on, day after summer day, among the purple foxgloves of the fields. At home voices began to grumble about the apparent stalemate, to complain that a combination of Axis supply and reinforcement with impossible terrain would enable the Germans to contain the invading forces. Ike was convinced that eventually Allied superiority in the air, on the sea and in gunfire would more than match the temporary German advantages. He kept the morale of his troops keyed up to continue their jabbing and punching.

Only on the extreme right was there a dashing success. General Collins' VII Corps attacked westward to cut the Normandy peninsula in two, isolating the port of Cherbourg. He fully lived up to his nickname, "Lightning Joe" Collins, by capturing the port on June 26th. The harbor was quickly restored through skillful use of deep-sea divers and minesweepers in a most hazardous mission.

Hitler had told his troops to stand or die, and they gave their all for Fuehrer and Fatherland. Fifty days after D-Day the Allied forces were still fighting doggedly along a line projected on the invasion plans for D-Day plus five.

Chasing the Enemy

In the grueling weeks after D-Day, the Allies slowly worked themselves into position. In spite of bad weather and unfavorable terrain, both the British and American forces steadily continued to build up strength. By July 9th the British and Canadians had finally taken Caen, making the outlook much brighter on the eastern flank. Then on July 18th the Americans moved into St. Lô, on the right flank.

As Eisenhower's chief of staff, Bedell Smith, has written:

. . . Now the Supreme Commander [Eisenhower]

could see an all-out, coordinated attack by the entire
Allied line which would at last put our forces in
decisive motion. He set up a small advance headquarters in Normandy, not far from Field Marshal
Montgomery. It was nothing but a forward base from
which he could visit the headquarters of his commanders but it was free from the flying limitations of
cross-Channel weather.

He was up and down the line like a football coach,
exhorting everyone to aggressive action. He constantly
urged his commanders to ask for full air support in
their drives. He demanded strong pressure against the
Germans at all times to keep the front in motion. . . .

The westward, or right-hand, side of the line was the
first to gather steam. Picking up momentum, the United
States First Army swung southward to the base of the
Cotentin Peninsula to attack the German armies from
the rear. Then on August 1st General Patton entered
the battle with the United States Third Army. A master
of mobile warfare, he was to operate on the First Army's
right flank. He also sent part of his troops (the VIII
Corps) to capture the Brittany Peninsula. By these
tactics the Americans hoped to encircle the German
forces, which were still concentrating their fire on the
Canadians and British in the Caen area.

The Germans struck back in a daring counterattack,
thinking they might be able to cut off the advancing
Americans. But the Americans held fast. The VIII
Corps, meanwhile, overran the Brittany Peninsula, and
the British and Canadians pressed forward from Caen.
The enemy spearhead was cut off and trapped west of

Br **2** *British Second Army*

Ca **1** *Canadian First Army*

US **1** *U.S. First Army*

US **3** *U.S. Third Army*

Cherbourg

English Channel

Le Havre

Carentan

Seine

Br **2**

Caen

St. Lô

Ca **1**

Falaise

Final Phase of the Normandy Campaign

US **1**

The encirclement of the Germans

US **3**

Le Mans

the Seine River. The German armies were a perfect target for the Allied bombers. Although German troops did manage to escape in fairly large numbers, eight enemy infantry divisions and two tank divisions were captured almost intact.

On swept the Allied forces over a mobile and widening front. The whole character of the fighting had now changed.

As Eisenhower struggled to provision his troops now that the Allied line of supply stretched long and disturbingly thin, he came up against a new problem. Churchill and he had been holding heated discussions over the merits of Operation Anvil-Dragoon, the plan for an invasion of southern France from the Mediterranean. Churchill wanted the forces destined for Dragoon diverted to Italy and the Balkans. He feared that a landing at Marseille would be extremely costly.

Eisenhower, however, wanted the port of Marseille for a quick, short route to build up his forces and supplies. Thirty-seven Allied divisions were to be in France by the end of August (twenty United States, twelve British, three Canadian, one French and one Polish). Each division used from six to seven hundred tons of supplies a day. Eisenhower regarded the capture of the magnificent ports of Marseille in southern France and Antwerp in Belgium as essential if the fast-moving charge was not to grind to a halt. He also wanted to free more of France to protect Patton's right flank.

Eisenhower suspected that Churchill really supported the Balkan campaign for political reasons—a desire to counter too great a Russian influence in that region. He therefore stubbornly persisted in his military opinion. At the same time he did inform Churchill that if the Prime Minister and President Roosevelt should finally decide on a Balkan campaign, he would of course follow through to the best of his military ability.

Eisenhower's naval aide, Captain Harry C. Butcher, later provided a vivid account of one of Ike and Churchill's stormy meetings:

> Ike said no, continued saying no all afternoon, and ended saying no in every form of the English language at his command. Ike lost the usual support of his former ally, his great friend Admiral Cunningham, who sided with the PM [Churchill], but General Ike had ardent backing from Admirals Ramsay and Tennant. Ike's position was that sound strategy called for making the Germans fight on as many fronts as possible. The landings in the Toulon area and advance up the Rhone Valley would further extend the enemy. . . .
>
> Ike argued so long and patiently that he was practically limp when the PM departed and observed that although he had said no in every language, the Prime Minister, undoubtedly, would return to the subject in two or three days and simply regard the issue as unsettled.

> . . . I told him that Admiral Tennant had taken me aside after the conference and said that Ike had been "sound at every step of the argument and thoroughly magnificent." A little later Admiral Ramsay telephoned me to add his appreciation of Ike's stalwartness.

Dragoon finally carried the day. On August 15, 1944, the amphibian boats crunched onto the beaches and put ashore the United States Seventh Army under Lieutenant General Alexander M. Patch, along with some paratroops, and units of the French First Army. These combined forces were known as the Sixth Army Group, with Lieutenant General Jacob L. Devers in

Churchill (left) and Ike take time out for a look at the famous "siren suit" the Prime Minister designed for getting into quickly during air raids.

command. A whirlwind campaign captured the naval base of Toulon and the port of Marseille. Then the Sixth Army Group swept up the Rhone valley to join with the United States Third Army under Patton at a junction north of Dijon by the middle of September.

In the north, the Allied divisions swirled across the Seine. As the machine of war rumbled toward Paris, the French forces of the Interior rose against the retreating Germans. Eisenhower had intended to by-pass the city of Paris itself, to keep it from being reduced to rubble, as had happened at Caen. But an uprising of Free French forces within the city forced him to

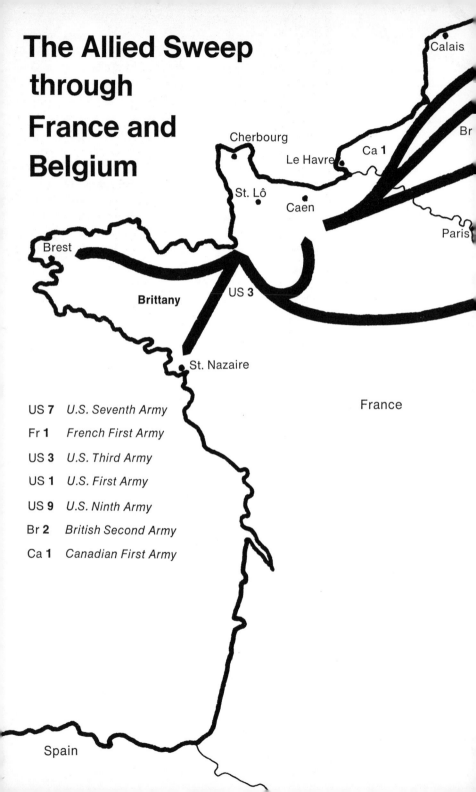

The Allied Sweep through France and Belgium

Calais

Br

Cherbourg

Le Havre

Ca **1**

St. Lô

Caen

Paris

Brest

Brittany

US **3**

St. Nazaire

France

US **7** *U.S. Seventh Army*

Fr **1** *French First Army*

US **3** *U.S. Third Army*

US **1** *U.S. First Army*

US **9** *U.S. Ninth Army*

Br **2** *British Second Army*

Ca **1** *Canadian First Army*

Spain

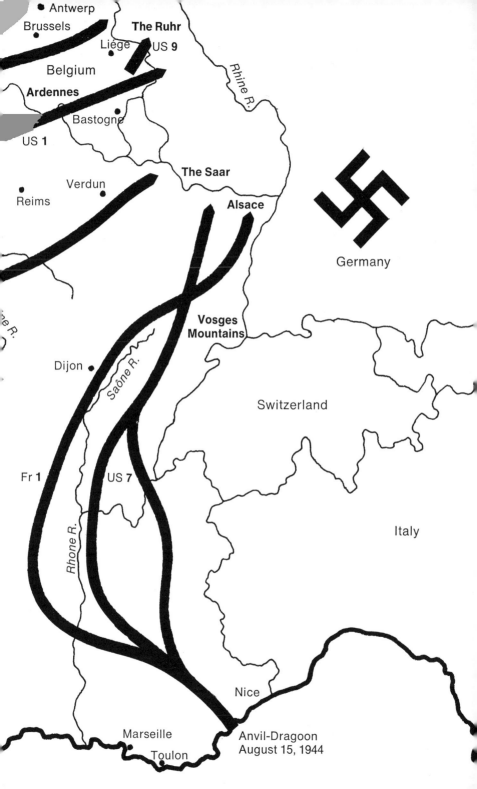

send in supporting troops. For the mission he chose General Le Clerc's French 2nd Division, backed up by the American 4th Division. The German garrison in Paris soon surrendered. Fortunately the damage to the city was not great.

General de Gaulle, established as head of the French government, requested the loan of American troops to ensure his position by a show of strength. Eisenhower had none to spare, but he sent two United States divisions to march down the boulevards—lined with cheering, delirious Parisians—on their way to the front. With typical modesty and diplomacy, Eisenhower declined to review the troops himself. He left that to Generals de Gaulle, Gerow and Bradley.

On flowed the stream of war, stretching to the utmost the Allied powers of supply. After a slow start the Allies had surpassed by far the projections made before D-Day. Their armies went plunging into Belgium, through the "black country" where coal is mined. Soon black, yellow and red-striped flags again flew triumphantly over the battered city of Brussels. And on September 4th Montgomery's forces dashed into Antwerp to find that the Germans had retreated so hurriedly they had carried out little destruction of the harbor. The approaches to the port, however, were still in enemy hands.

In early September Eisenhower paid one of his frequent visits to the front lines. On his return to headquarters, his plane had to make a forced landing.

The Supreme Allied Commander arrives in a jeep at a front-line position "somewhere in France."

As he himself has described the incident:

> Caught in a sudden storm, we found it impossible to return to our own little landing strip near headquarters and had no place to land except on a neighboring beach . . . we tried to pull the plane far enough away from the water's edge to prevent its inundation by the rising tide. In doing so, I badly wrenched my knee. My pilot . . . helped me across the beach while I kept an anxious eye on the smooth sand in front of us for any telltale signs of buried explosives. We reached a country road and started the long trek toward headquarters. It was a miserable walk through a driving rain but we had little hope of thumbing a ride because the back road we were

traveling was rarely used by our soldiers. However, within a few minutes there came up behind us a jeep into which eight soldiers had managed to crowd.

We flagged them down and the occupants, instantly recognizing me, jumped out to help. They were obviously astounded to see the commanding general in such an out-of-the-way place and limping along in the rain. I asked them to take me to headquarters and so great was their concern that they practically lifted me into the front seat of the jeep . . . they allowed no one else except the driver to sit in front. I still do not understand how all the rest of them piled in and on the jeep and managed to get my pilot aboard, but this they did.

Eisenhower's associates frequently tried to persuade him to give up these continual visits to the front-line areas, but he refused. He believed that the fighting men needed to feel that their commanders were solidly behind them. Whenever possible he took time to question the enlisted men and find out what they were thinking and doing. Nothing, he felt, could be more important to the war effort than keeping up the morale of the combat troops.

By October of 1944 the Allied armies were crowding the German borders. Fifty-four divisions now lined the front—a total more than matched, however, by German ground strength. Allied supplies were short, and the worst floods in decades turned the inferior roads into muddy swamps, kept the air forces grounded, and made life miserable for the infantry. But Ike still decided to press the offensive before the Germans could reorganize and while winter was still only threatening.

The goal was firmly in mind: to destroy enemy troops. Ike insisted once again that Germany's great fight would come west of the Rhine. He sparked a major drive in the south, where Patton's Third Army leaped to the attack on November 8th. By the middle of November they crossed the German frontier to confront the strong Saar Valley defenses. General Devers, in a supporting movement, stepped up his efforts to get through the tree-topped Vosges Mountains and over to the plains of Alsace, thus attacking the Saar Valley from the south.

Another major effort gathered momentum to the north, where Montgomery struggled to drive the enemy out of the islands that guarded the approaches to Antwerp. By November 9th these German strongholds had been eliminated. Quickly the port was cleared of mines, and by November 26th it was receiving supplies.

On November 15th Montgomery headed eastward. Below him General Bradley renewed the attack toward the Ruhr valley with the United States First Army and the new Ninth Army. By December 3rd the Americans had come up against the Roer River. Here the Germans controlled the area by means of the great Schmidt dams upriver. These could be opened to flood the invading troops below should they get too belligerent. The First Army settled down to batter at the dam's defenses.

All along the line there was mud-slow slugging, with the infantry creeping forward on artillery and sheer will power. In the bad season only the infantry could operate, and their continued losses greatly weakened the Allied units. Men from supply were thrown into the fray, and General Carl Spaatz of the Air Forces even gave 10,000 men from his bomber command. Green troops were rushed across the Atlantic, supposedly to rotate with tired and tense veterans. But few veterans could be spared. The mud-stained uniforms stayed in the line beside the new. Morale was a constant problem. The muddy war, with its slow gains and increasing fatigue along the long, long Allied line, brought home the exposed and lonely position each soldier faced.

Eisenhower thinned out to skeletal strength the forces in the center, Ardennes section of the line. This enabled him to bolster the attacks on the Roer dams and the Saar Valley. He realized that there was a risk, for the Germans might decide to attack toward weakness. The Supreme Commander knew that they had reserves they could use for just that purpose. But he also knew, and General Bradley supported him, that the strong troops on either side of the Ardennes sector could execute a pincer movement should such an attack occur. This, plus air support, could prevent any really disastrous enlargement of an attack.

Thus Eisenhower somberly faced his fourth Christmas at war—with his troops toe to toe with the Germans along the Siegfried West Wall and a dangerously thinned-out line in the central Ardennes sector.

Hitler's Desperate Gamble
– the Battle of the Bulge

On the morning of December 16, 1944, roaring cannons along a seventy-five mile front sounded the first warning of a massive German counteroffensive. Out of the early morning darkness, German infantrymen supported by lunging tanks began smashing through American lines in the Ardennes Forest area.

This surprise counterattack had been conceived by Hitler himself, and the entire scheme had been planned with the greatest adroitness and resourcefulness. In utmost secrecy the German high command had withdrawn battle-weary but experienced divisions of high quality from the western defense line. These they

Adolf Hitler (back to camera) talks to General Gerd von Rund-stedt.

had regrouped and reoutfitted far from the eye of the prying enemy. Tanks and artillery were thriftily hoarded, and first-rate tank units were held in reserve for a bold, determined use at the proper time and place. Some of the best German commanders assumed command, including the brilliant German field marshal, Gerd von Rundstedt.

At first, no one high or low in the chain of Allied command fully comprehended the giant scope of the German counteroffensive. Both Eisenhower and Bradley had expected that the Germans would make one last stab before withdrawing into their homeland. And Allied Intelligence had noted that a number of infantry and tank divisions were quietly and mysteriously withdrawing from the more active front-line combat areas.

Still, there were many elements that led to the Allies' being taken by surprise. One was the optimism reflected in many commanders' field reports. Another was the clever concealment of the German preparations and the fact that Eisenhower thought the Ardennes sector highly difficult physical terrain for a major German attack. Finally, there was the lack of Allied aerial reconnaissance. Fog and persistent bad weather had limited to five the number of reconnaissance missions flown between December 5th and 16th.

Even when the Germans actually struck, in the cold pre-dawn gloom of December 16th, the Allies could not be certain that the enemy was launching a major offensive. By this time American troops were used to small German units probing here and there for soft spots in the line. Later, as advance enemy patrols started to seal off American units in the sparsely held sector at the north end of the line, communications became disrupted. Hour by hour, communication between the Allied armies became more confused or entirely cut off.

Within forty-eight hours German armor had made two huge penetrations in the American lines, and *Wehrmacht* columns were sweeping ahead in their desperate drive toward the Meuse River. The Meuse was the real objective, which the German commanders had sworn to reach at all costs. Essentially their strategy called for a mighty counteroffensive along fifty miles of a seventy-five-mile front. The critical blows were to hit the Allied line at the center. Of course there was a danger in such an attack. If the German flanks were not amply secured, the Allied defenders would be able to close off the center salient with a pincers movement. But this was a gamble the Germans were prepared to take.

The Germans executed their surprise attack with stunning swiftness. It inflicted shattering losses and personal suffering on the American armies in the field, and it had a most depressive effect upon civilians at home. For the blow fell on the eve of the Christmas season, just when people were beginning to believe that the war would soon be over.

But the sudden German counterattack failed to alarm Ike. In fact he said afterward that he hadn't been really scared until he caught up with the headlines of the American newspapers two weeks later. When word first came of the German breakthrough, Eisenhower was with General Bradley discussing replacement problems. At first no one realized how much power was behind the German drive, but Ike did order Bradley to send two armored divisions to the attack area. He felt certain that this was no local attack, but bad weather continued to keep Allied planes grounded. There was no possibility of getting an aerial view of German movements.

Not until the morning of the 17th did Allied commanders become painfully aware of what they were up against. Information began to pour in from captured Germans and Allied Intelligence agencies. It confirmed

US **1**   *U.S. First Army*

US **3**   *U.S. Third Army*

Liége

US **1**

Meuse R.

Malmédy

Belgium

St. Vith

Houffalize

Ardennes

Germany

Bastogne

US **3**

US **3**

Sedan

France

Luxembourg

The Battle of the Bulge

December 16, 1944, to January 16, 1945

Route of the German attack

Direction of U.S. counterattack

Area of German penetration

beyond question that the Germans had made deep penetrations in several spots. They were now on the verge of breaking into the clear if the Allied lines were not immediately reinforced.

Unfortunately SHAEF had not yet been able to build up much in the way of reserve forces. On the morning of December 17th, Eisenhower had only two divisions immediately available. Both the 82nd and 101st Airborne divisions were recovering and re-equipping in training camps near Reims, France, after the hard fighting they had encountered in a parachute drop in Holland. They were quickly reinforced with additional artillery and antitank guns. Then the 101st Airborne was rushed in trucks to the beleaguered city of Bastogne, while the 82nd Airborne was directed farther north near St. Vith. Arrangements were also made to bring up the 11th Armored Division, which had just arrived from England, and to transfer the 17th Airborne to France.

Meanwhile the German juggernaut continued to roll forward toward the Meuse Valley. French liaison officers were wringing their hands and saying that it looked as if the 1940 German smash at Sedan would happen all over again. It was now completely clear to all commanders that the Germans had thrown into the attack the largest concentration of armored divisions since the Normandy days.

All day through December 18th, reports spilled into Supreme Headquarters at Versailles of new German advances moving steadily through rain and fog. On the 19th Eisenhower and Air Chief Marshal Tedder went to Verdun to confer with Generals Bradley, Patton and Devers. There they agreed unanimously that the Allies should counterattack as soon as possible.

Eisenhower believed that if they moved quickly and forcefully they could turn the German breakthrough into a great Allied opportunity. The counterattack need not begin on both flanks simultaneously. Before this crisis, Patton's forces had been scheduled to drive eastward in an attempt to crack the German west wall. Thus they could quickly be diverted north to hit the Germans on their southern flank. December 22nd or 23rd was set as the date for Patton's three-division attack.

When Eisenhower returned from his morning meeting at Verdun, he heard the chilling news that German forces were striking out fast to threaten St. Vith, Houffalize and Bastogne. The possibilities were fearsome to contemplate. It became obvious that the enemy had as his ultimate targets four areas, all critical to the Allied effort: the vital port of Antwerp through which supplies had to flow; British advance bases at Antwerp and Brussels; the city of Liége with its crucial road and rail center heavily stocked with supplies; and the vital communication lines linking Antwerp to Louvain to Liége. The Allies must hold these targets at all cost.

At this point the Allied Commander in Chief made another major decision. Knowing that the heaviest attack was in the north, where it imperiled both the American and British armies, Ike split the battlefield right up the middle of the breakthrough area. Montgomery was given command of all forces north of the German bulge and Bradley command of those to the south. Dividing the battlefield seemed essential to Eisenhower for a number of reasons. First, he thought it most important psychologically that Bradley's head-quarters not be shifted from the city of Luxembourg. Any transfer would be bad for morale, besides upsetting staff work generally. Ike was also worried about the problem of communication between General Bradley on the southeastern end of the German bulge and General Hodges and the United States First Army on the northern side of the enemy breakthrough.

For eight crucial days the violent German offensive spread havoc and confusion through the Allied armies. Undermanned troops struggled desperately in mud and snow to recover their balance after successive shock waves of German armor hit them.

In the nightmare of broken communications, forward units were unable to keep in touch with their sup-porting forces to the rear. Rumor fed upon rumor. Roads became clogged, and often highly valuable guns and equipment were abandoned unnecessarily. Or were discarded without having been made unusable. Yet the Battle of the Bulge was not simply an epic tale of Allied rout and recovery. From the very outbreak, small bands of fighters dug in to make heroic stands—often without knowledge of the total situation and frequently without sufficient equipment and rein-forcements.

American troops held superbly on both shoulders of the German drive—on the northern flank and farther west where German advances were actually halted.

On the southern flank the American armies also held ground gamely or made slight gains. And at Bastogne, the key to the southern Ardennes, the American forces put up a heroic defense. The little town came to symbolize the gallant stand of the American troops in the Battle of the Bulge. Entirely surrounded shortly after the beginning of this battle, the Bastogne defenders stood off the Germans against tremendous odds. The relief that came to the besieged defenders by airlift was the largest demonstration of air supply during wartime that had ever been made. During four days more than eight hundred giant cargo-carrying C-47s dropped supplies. In addition fifty gliders carrying medical personnel for the wounded were landed safely within the encircled town.

At the outset of the German counterattack, wretched

A giant C-47 drops supplies over Bastogne (December 23, 1944).

weather had grounded Allied planes for several days. But on December 23rd the weather changed, and stupendous air attacks began seriously to nettle German troops. Each day thereafter, Allied planes destroyed much of the enemy's transport and fuel supply, inflicting losses the Germans could ill afford if the attack was to keep rolling.

On December 25th Hitler received the worst possible news. One of his favorite generals, Alfred Jodl, told him that the German forces could not possibly force their way to the Meuse River. They must abandon all thought of crossing the Meuse in favor of a battle east of the river. This was a bitter decision, for by now elements of the German forces were within four miles of the Meuse. And the German generals knew the river had immense value for the Allies, either as a permanent defense line or as a springboard for a further drive toward Germany.

On December 28th, for the first time in twelve days, the Germans failed to advance at all. And Patton's Third Army was now attacking to the south. Again on December 29th the German war machine failed to make any advances whatever against the Allied lines. And the United States Third Army, bolstered by strong armor reinforcements, advanced a mile at several points inflicting heavy punishment on the enemy. Now the German position began to look quite different. Instead of reaching the Meuse River in three days in a break-through surge of power, the enemy was four miles short on the twelfth day. Instead of expanding his fifty-mile spearhead as the attack pressed westward, he was forced to contract his forces.

Initially the enemy penetration was on a fifty-mile front. But it was imperative for the Germans to pull their flanking columns along as the drive rolled westward. And for the Allies it was vital to keep the enemy's spearhead from widening. Right from the early stages, the Allies hoped that the massive attack would overreach itself, enabling them to take advantage of the situation by encircling the enemy and destroying huge quantities of men and equipment.

As matters turned out, the enemy's only conspicuous success was the rapid thrust of his middle column straight west. Unfortunately the Germans never succeeded in pulling their flanking columns along with them. Thus they dared not penetrate too far until their flanks were secure. And this security they were never able to achieve.

The great counteroffensive of the Allied forces began on January 3, 1945. Under General Montgomery, American First Army troops began counterattacking from the north toward Houffalize, which was in the center of the bulge. Six days later, after Patton's tanks had battered their way into Bastogne, his Third Army forces continued their drive toward Houffalize from the south. The weather was unbelievably bad. Snow was waist high in many places; temperatures hovered close to zero. The roads were icy and cluttered with mired equipment abandoned by the retreating Germans. But the enemy continued to fight fiercely. Some of the heaviest fighting of the entire Battle of the Bulge took place in the Bastogne area during the following week.

On January 9th Patton's armies knocked out the last German resistance at Bastogne. All along the line Allied armies pressed ahead. Then on January 12th the worst German fears were realized. The long-awaited Russian winter offensive broke out in the east. At this news Hitler immediately ordered the entire Sixth Panzer Army to the Eastern Front. By January 16th the two American forces joined at Houffalize, and the last phase of the historic battle was soon over.

It had lasted scarcely a month. But it had brought together in mortal combat more than twenty German and, eventually, over thirty Allied divisions. It had dealt a crippling blow to the German war machine, but in the short space of a month the Americans had suffered 76,890 casualties (8,607 killed, 47,139 wounded and 21,144 missing). The Germans, however, suffered an estimated 120,000 serious casualties, and they had to abandon quantities of invaluable equipment and supplies. Hitler had lost his desperate gamble.

During the crisis Eisenhower had once again demonstrated his talents for organizing his team of commanders and forces and inspiring them to work together splendidly under the most stressful conditions. The final outcome was a great tribute to his leadership. It was also an immortal tribute to the heroic efforts and high quality of his troops. In the long story of American military history, the Battle of the Bulge will always stand as a shining chapter.

Victory in Europe

Some bitter fighting still faced the Allies in Europe, but they knew now that it would be in the nature of an epilogue. Germany was stumbling beneath a rain of blows. On the Eastern Front the Russians were driving into Poland and Czechoslovakia. By February 20th they would be some sixty miles from Berlin.

On the Western Front Eisenhower had his forces poised for the final grand campaign. Meanwhile the Allied air forces were overwhelmingly engaged in bombing any remaining German hopes into rubble. Once more Ike had to uphold his strategy in the face of opposition. This time it was General Sir Alan

Brooke, Chief of the British Imperial General Staff, who challenged Eisenhower's plan for an advance on all fronts. Field Marshal Brooke believed that the Allied forces were not strong enough to attack at more than one point. All the other parts of the line, he maintained, should remain in strong defensive positions.

Eisenhower, on the other hand, was convinced that once the Allies had advanced to the west bank of the Rhine, they could throw as many as seventy-five strong divisions against the enemy provided they attacked on a more widely spread-out front.

In late January of 1945 there was a conference of heads of state and military commanders on the island of Malta. Here Eisenhower's plans for a full-scale drive won full support. (Later Field Marshal Brooke was to say, "Thank God, Ike, you stuck by your plan.")

On February 8th Montgomery started his Canadians slogging determinedly through the mud. During the first week of March they converged with the American Ninth Army on the west bank of the Rhine. From here they could look grimly across the great river at the smoky cluster of cities which make up the industrial Ruhr region.

Success smiled all down the line. Devers' troops forged forward in the south, and in the center Bradley's First Army hammered its way into Cologne. On March 7th one detachment from the 9th Armored Division, rushing up quickly to the Ludendorff Bridge at Remagen, found complete confusion among the

The Ludendorff Bridge over the Rhine at Remagen, photographed shortly after its unexpected capture by the 9th Armored Division.

Germans responsible for destroying the bridge. As a result the Americans were able to swarm over it and save it from destruction. Bradley exuberantly called Ike, and Eisenhower urged him to exploit this rare good fortune and throw across everything he had.

As the Supreme Commander's official driver, WAC Lieutenant Kay Summersby, later reported the incident:

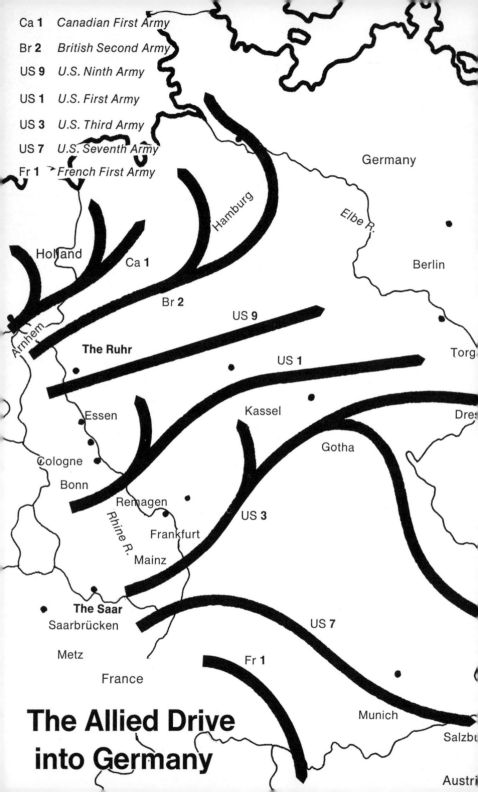

Ca 1   *Canadian First Army*
Br 2   *British Second Army*
US 9   *U.S. Ninth Army*
US 1   *U.S. First Army*
US 3   *U.S. Third Army*
US 7   *U.S. Seventh Army*
Fr 1   *French First Army*

Germany

Elbe R.

Berlin

Holland

Ca 1

Hamburg

Br 2

US 9

Arnhem

The Ruhr

US 1

Torg

Essen

Kassel

Dres

Cologne

Gotha

Bonn

Remagen

Rhine R.

Frankfurt

US 3

Mainz

The Saar

Saarbrücken

US 7

Metz

France

Fr 1

Munich

Salzb

The Allied Drive
into Germany

Austri

This was a superb example of General Eisenhower's active, literal, field command of the war, a typical answer to uninformed critics who accused him of being a red-tape general completely out of touch with the actual fighting. Bradley already had begun exploitation of the bridge, but he called to get Ike's concurrence. The Germans had presented them with one of the choice plums of war; should they junk present plans and risk throwing everything into the bridgehead? General Ike acted with a born soldier's lightning-fast decision: grab it, pour in everything we have, get not less than five divisions across as soon as possible.

Patton threw a second bridgehead across on the more southerly sector on March 22nd. By the twenty-fifth of that month the triumphant Allies held the west bank of the Rhine, even to the sticky Saar Basin.

A brooding, despondent Hitler, in striving to stave off ruin, floundered wildly. He relieved the able von Rundstedt and brought Field Marshal Albert von Kessel- · ring up from Italy. But the German army was being chewed to pieces. At times 10,000 prisoners a day were pouring into the hands of Allied forces.

On March 23rd and 24th, from a lookout high on a hill, the Supreme Commander watched the first of the seven great Allied armies span the last defense of the Fatherland—the noble, fast-flowing Rhine. Back in the States there was now a great clamor for a speedy rush to Berlin. But Eisenhower stood firm. He refused to divert supplies and slow down the rest of his forces in order to support one grand push for a city three hundred miles away. He was determined to divide the German

Yanks and Russians clasp hands at Torgau.

forces and overrun the whole country as soon as possible.

By April 1st, a double envelopment by Montgomery's and Bradley's forces surrounded the Ruhr Valley. By the eighteenth of April that forging ground of German armaments had surrendered. In the meantime Bradley's forces had reorganized and streaked for the Elbe River. They joined with the Russians at Torgau on April 25th, dividing Germany neatly in two. Devers' American and French armies poured into Austria. And in the north

Montgomery isolated the German forces occupying Denmark.

One memorable and tragic day for Eisenhower during this period was April 12th, which he spent with General Patton. They began by viewing a hidden hoard of German art treasures, and gold bars worth perhaps $250,000,000. These Nazi treasures had been buried in a deep salt mine. Eisenhower and Patton then went on to the prison camp at Gotha, a storehouse of horrors equal to the dreadful concentration camps at Dachau and Belsen. So that there would be no later doubt of the truth of that grisly site, Eisenhower immediately cabled Washington and London to send editors and representative government groups to view such concentration camps.

Late that night came the most shattering news of all. President Franklin D. Roosevelt had died of a stroke in Warm Springs, Georgia.

On the last day of the same month, in a small room deep in a network of bunkers under the Reich Chancellery in Berlin, another war leader met his death. In the company of the woman he had married just the day before, Adolf Hitler shot himself. His wife had taken poison. An orderly then quickly removed the bodies to a courtyard above. There gasoline was poured over them and set aflame to prevent their bodies from falling into the hands of the Russians, now fighting in the very streets of Berlin.

Admiral Karl Doenitz inherited what little authority was left in Germany. But the various armies had already begun to surrender—in Italy, Austria and Scandinavia. Doenitz and other Germans, strongest in their hatred of the Russians, wished to surrender only on the Western Front. Eisenhower, acting on concerted Allied plans, insisted that they surrender to all the victors, including Russia, and do so unconditionally. At 2:41 A.M. on May 7, 1945, at General Eisenhower's headquarters in Reims, Doenitz' representatives signed the surrender instrument, to be ratified two days later at the Russian headquarters in Berlin. While quiet descended over Germany, a roar of exultation sped round a joyous world.

From Morningside Heights to NATO

On July 2, 1945, a throng of four million cheered Ike along a triumphant, thirty-seven-mile motorcade through New York. At Washington, D. C., the day before, another riotous reception had greeted him; there more than a million people turned out to cheer. Everywhere the nation wanted to see him; hear him.

In a speech delivered at West Point Eisenhower showed his growing concern that the wartime allies should have become so quickly quarrelsome. "If we stick together we can lick anybody we have to fight. If we stick together intelligently we won't have to fight."

In Abilene, where his homecoming brought together

seventy-five Eisenhowers, who occupied an entire floor of the hotel, he struck another theme: the necessity of pushing forward the boundaries of education so that our youth would develop "a grasp upon government and on things that are vital in our national life."

It was apparent that his mind at this time was very much preoccupied with the possibility of playing some new role in the field of education. He was deeply convinced that education, properly directed, could bring about a clearer understanding of the individual's role in a free society. And thus it could promote both democracy and peace among nations.

Meanwhile, however, General Marshall was retiring as chief of staff, and on November 20, 1945, President Harry S. Truman appointed Eisenhower to the post. Once more Ike was cast into the eye of the hurricane. For the next two years he found himself astride three complex problems: demobilization, the unification of the armed forces into a single national defense establishment, and a noisy insistent clamor that he permit himself to be drafted for the presidency. The latter two problems were particularly vexing.

With the lessons of World War II behind, and the fearful uncertainties of developing world tensions ahead, Congress began a drastic overhaul of the nation's defense machinery. The goal was the merging of the Army, Navy and the Air Force into a single department of defense. Interservice rivalries broke into the open, and there began a bitter battle between the branches, particularly behind the scenes. Congress sought to bring

Enthusiastic throngs shower ticker tape on General Eisenhower during a triumphant motorcade through New York City.

about unification by passing the National Security Act of 1947. But this Act, which brought three services under one Department of Defense did not submerge interservice antagonisms by any stretch of the imagination. Eisenhower threw himself into the difficult task with every resource he had. His presence as chief of staff at this critical juncture was most important to the eventual acceptance of the unification effort.

The matter of discouraging those who wanted Eisenhower to run for president of the United States was also difficult. Even before the General returned from Europe, public opinion polls showed Ike to be a certain winner if he entered the presidential lists. Moreover, as 1948 approached, he was being courted by different groups in both major parties. To forestall these efforts he issued a strong statement in January, 1948, refusing to permit his name to be entered in the New Hampshire presidential primary. "I am not available for and could not accept nomination to high political office." Professional soldiers, he added, should "in the absence of some obvious and overriding reason, abstain from seeking high political office."

Two weeks later he went on leave from his post as chief of staff, and soon began the tremendous task of writing his wartime memoirs, *Crusade in Europe*. Working furiously from extensive notes and other materials, he dictated and revised this 200,000-word manuscript in five weeks—an incredible feat for turning out this amount of copy.

While debating what to do next, Eisenhower considered a job in industry, but rejected the idea because it would not be "fitting for me to use the name I have made in the service of my country for private profit."

Eisenhower's interest in education became clearly evident with the announcement of his appointment as president of Columbia University. He was formally installed in this post on Columbus Day, 1948. One of his first steps at Columbia was to rebuild the university's financial status, which had slumped through several years of deficit operations.

Even in his new position on the campus at Morningside Heights, Eisenhower was still harassed by requests for advice on national security. Secretary of Defense James Forrestal, who was still very much involved with unification difficulties, secured Eisenhower as his senior military adviser. And throughout his entire service at Columbia, Ike was constantly being summoned to Washington for consultation on military matters.

At Columbia he took no salary for his duties, and he often worked fifteen hours a day. It was a rare day that did not bring in two hundred or more invitations to speak. One outburst of criticism was fired at him for accepting a grant from Communist Poland to finance Polish studies at Columbia, but Ike brushed this off decisively. He insisted that a university must stand as a citadel of freedom and that we must learn everything we can about peoples and their ideas in the world about us.

Barely two years after Eisenhower had gone to Columbia, he had thrust upon him an entirely new kind of assignment. On December 19, 1950, President

As president of Columbia University, Eisenhower tours the campus with a group of visiting foreign students.

Truman appointed Ike as Supreme Commander for the military forces of the North Atlantic Treaty Organization (NATO). Officially this organization was designed as a collective defense pact among the countries of the North Atlantic area, but practically it was created in response to an ever increasing danger of Soviet penetration into Western Europe. Under the agreement any attack upon any country belonging to the organization was to be considered as an "attack against them all."

Clearly this was a new and bold venture for the United States. In joining NATO, the United States was abandoning a 160-year-old tradition against alliances with European military powers.

Eisenhower plunged with renewed energy into this assignment of creating a collective security system almost out of a vacuum. He began by flying to Europe and visiting the capitals of every European nation within three weeks. Then after a quick return visit to the United States to report to the President and Congress and arrange a leave of absence from his duties at Columbia, he returned to Europe. There he spent the next fifteen months building the defensive forces of Western Europe.

By 1952 NATO had taken impressive strides in overcoming national rivalries, personal jealousies and distrust, and in building an integrated defense plan for the whole of Western and Southeastern Europe. The military assistance program for Western Europe had become an established fact.

Once again as the nation moved toward another presidential campaign the press began chanting for Ike. All during the summer and fall of 1951, prominent political leaders paid visits to him at his headquarters outside Paris. By the end of the year Ike's future plans had developed into a supermarket of rumors.

Finally, on January 6, 1952, Senator Henry Cabot Lodge of Massachusetts held a press conference in Washington to make a dramatic announcement: General Eisenhower's name would be entered in the New Hampshire presidential primary in March, he said. Asked if he had Ike's permission, he declared emphatically: "I will not be repudiated."

"We Want Ike"

On March 11, 1952, the state of New Hampshire held its primary election. Despite ice, rain and snow a record turnout voted overwhelmingly for Eisenhower as their Republican presidential candidate. It was an amazing achievement. A man who had not campaigned, was not even in the country, and had never publicly declared to which party he belonged, had won the first state presidential primary of 1952. And he had defeated a most formidable and respected opponent— Senator Robert A. Taft. Taft had campaigned hard, and his friends had organized a major effort to heave him into the presidency.

Just one week later, in the Midwest, a second surprise stumped the political experts. Some called it the "Minnesota Miracle." Here the Eisenhower enthusiasts had been unable to secure the General's permission to file his name in the state presidential primary. And because of legal technicalities, they had been thwarted in their attempt to enter his name by petition. Nevertheless, at the last moment they decided to organize a "write in" campaign.

Their prospects were not good. Former Minnesota Governor Harold Stassen was on the ballot as a "favorite son," and he was strongly favored to win. In addition, primary election day—March 18—was wet and slushy. The voting officials were predicting a very low turnout.

Governor Sherman Adams of New Hampshire helps set up an Eisenhower-for-President headquarters at Concord.

By noon they knew better. From all parts of the state came frantic calls from polling places that had run out of ballots. Hurriedly the Minnesota secretary of state ruled that ballots would be legal if written on plain paper and initialed by the election judges. In cities where voting machines rather than paper ballots were in use, election authorities fumbled with metal plates. These had to be removed so that insistent voters could write in, however clumsily, the name of the man they wanted for president. When the results were tallied, there were 109,000 write-ins for Eisenhower. This was short of the 129,000 votes for Stassen, of course, but it revealed an incredible burst of popularity in view of the agonizing frustrations of not even being on the ballot.

From his headquarters in France, Eisenhower said he was truly "astonished." Then he added that "the mounting number of my fellow citizens who are voting to make me the Republican nominee [for President] are forcing me to reëxamine my present and past decisions."

Minnesota proved to be the real shot in the arm that the "draft Eisenhower" forces needed in the race for the presidential nomination. On May 31st Ike left France for Washington, where he resigned his Army commission. Then he moved on to Abilene, his boyhood home, where he delivered his first political speech.

Politics boiled furiously during the next few months as the contest between Ike and Taft seesawed back and forth right down to convention time in early July. By the time Eisenhower left his Denver headquarters to go to the Republican National Convention at Chicago, he

Ike sits with his fingers crossed during an informal news conference aboard the special train taking him from Denver to the Republican National Convention in Chicago.

and Taft were running neck and neck—Taft with slightly more than five hundred pledged delegates, Eisenhower with somewhat fewer than five hundred. Six hundred and four were needed to win.

On the third day of the convention, the climactic moment finally arrived. At the end of the first roll call, Ike led Taft 595 to 500. Suddenly the Minnesota standard began to bobble wildly to attract the attention of the Chairman. Above the din Senator Edward Thye called out, "Minnesota wishes to change its vote to Eisenhower." That was it. The first great stride toward the White House had now reached firm dry ground.

Eisenhower's first act was to hurry over to Taft's headquarters. There he expressed his esteem for his defeated opponent and pledged to work with him if elected. Richard Nixon was his first choice for a running mate, and his name was immediately approved.

Returning to Denver Eisenhower began to prepare at once for his first real participation in national politics. It was a whirlwind experience—quite unlike any he had engaged in before. Between July 11th, when he was nominated, and November 4th, election day, he traveled more than 50,000 miles and delivered more than 200 speeches. He took advice from the experienced politicians on matters affecting the organization of the campaign against his Democratic rival, Adlai Stevenson. But he also made it clear that he intended to follow his own instincts no matter how unorthodox they might appear politically.

Adopting a mildly progressive course, Eisenhower insisted that he would not turn the clock back if elected, that he would support and extend domestic legislation like social security. But he struck out against the seemingly boundless bureaucracy which seemed to be developing at the national level. He felt the federal government was absorbing more and more of the functions of local government. He also hammered away at excessive taxation. He believed that it smothered incentive. Much of his campaign was also devoted to attacks on inflation.

In foreign affairs, he charged that mismanagement had weakened the United States position with regard to her allies. And in a dramatic moment during a Detroit speech he announced that if elected he would go to Korea. The implication here was clear that he would attempt to end this indecisive conflict which had been undertaken by the United Nations against the Communists. The Korean War had inflicted severe casualties on American forces. It had become a protracted struggle that was causing bitter and rising resentment in the United States.

On election day, even before UNIVAC, the electronic brain, began to register its cold calculations of election trends, it was obvious that a smashing victory was in the making. From north and south, east and west, the results tumbled in, all pointing to a landslide. Final result: Eisenhower was the victor by a six-and-one-half-million popular majority. He carried 39 states and won 442 electoral votes to Stevenson's 89.

Elated with the results, Ike and Mamie joined the celebrants for a brief period, then slipped out to find their car for the ride back to Morningside Heights, where Ike still resided as president of Columbia. A shock awaited them as they climbed into the waiting limousine. The driver who had brought them was no longer at the wheel. Two total strangers—Secret Service men—sat in the front seat.

Late in November the President-elect carried out in

Dwight Eisenhower and his wife, Mamie, wave to their cheering supporters after hearing the news that Ike has been elected president.

great secrecy his campaign promise to visit Korea. For twenty-four hours no word was given on his departure. He landed in Korea on December 2nd.

For two weeks Ike examined at first hand conditions in Korea and the Far East. Then he returned to New York for an intensive series of conferences on appointments to his cabinet and plans for his new administration.

Beginning his inaugural address with a brief prayer which he had composed himself, Dwight Eisenhower, 34th President of the United States, hit hardest on a note that would ring out throughout his eight years in the presidency. It must be "the supreme purpose of all free men," he said, "to save humanity from preying upon itself."

The office Eisenhower now entered had long been known for its great burdens. But even the great institution of the presidency had undergone vast change. Twenty years before Ike delivered his inaugural address, President Hoover had tried in vain to persuade Congress to give him five secretaries instead of three. By 1952 the White House Staff and Special Projects Personnel numbered more than 200 and would soon expand to 275. And not only had new responsibilities been added to the office of president, but even the old ones had expanded.

In Theodore Roosevelt's day the United States maintained diplomatic relations with fifty countries. During the Eisenhower Administration this number topped one hundred. Washington, D. C., was becoming more and more the crossroads for chiefs of state, with twenty-six kings, prime ministers or other heads of state visiting the nation's capital in a single year.

In the area of national safety, of course, the responsibilities of the new president pressed upon him with greater urgency than ever before. The threat of nuclear attack and push-button nuclear warfare placed the President, as commander in chief, in a far more sensitive position than formerly. During the Eisenhower Administration, for the first time in American history, the President could order and bring about the destruction of cities, and even nations, within the span of an hour.

Eisenhower brought to the office of president the working habits, experience and concept of leadership that had evolved over a lifetime. He placed great responsibility upon his key staff at the White House and took for granted enormous sacrifice. His own personal secretary, Ann Whitman, whose superb managerial talents and speed created a White House legend, was always at her desk before 7:30 A.M. She rarely left before 8:00 P.M., and after leaving she usually received several more calls with regard to additional office details. She also spent almost every Saturday, Sunday and other holidays on the job.

One of President Eisenhower's sharpest departures from tradition was the staff system he set up in the White House. He created the office of assistant to the president and encouraged this aide, former Governor Sherman Adams, to act as the nerve center for sorting out and reducing policy conflicts to as few areas of agreement and disagreement as possible. Ike preferred his top staff aides to thrash out policy differences among themselves and his Cabinet members or other officials involved. Only then were they to present him with the areas of agreement or disagreement and the alternatives in the disputed areas.

Although this system was criticized on the grounds that sometimes important matters may be decided at the subordinate level without presidential participation, subsequent experience seems to have brought support for many of the staff organizational methods Eisenhower employed while he was in the White House. Reviewing these methods in the light of later experience, a distinguished English scholar at Oxford remarked that, while the Eisenhower system may have eliminated "too much decision making from the very top, it did mean that people in government knew what was going on and that government officials were not by-passed without a chance to participate in decisions directly concerning their office."

More than any other recent president, he tried to elevate the Cabinet as an advisory body. He looked upon his Cabinet as a body of advisers who ought to review every important question not concerned with confidential security matters. Cabinet meetings were held weekly throughout his entire administration. To emphasize the importance he gave them, he created a Cabinet Secretariat to prepare agendas, circulate position papers in advance, and to keep track of all decisions and how well they were followed up. Several weeks after Eisenhower's inauguration the Department of Health, Education, and Welfare was set up. Mrs. Oveta Culp Hobby was appointed the first secretary of this department.

Eisenhower also began at once to make the National Security Council into a top policy agency of the executive branch of government. (It had not been a very instrumental agency since its creation in 1947.) NSC meetings were held every Thursday morning to discuss security matters of the highest priority. Soon this agency was playing an extremely influential role in the

The President meets with his Cabinet. Left to right: Secretary of Labor, James P. Mitchell; Postmaster General, Arthur Summerfield; Secretary of State, John Foster Dulles; President Eisenhower; Secretary of Defense, Charles Wilson; Secretary of Agriculture, Ezra Taft Benson. Foreground (backs to the camera): Secretary of Health, Education, and Welfare, Oveta Culp Hobby; Secretary of Commerce, Sinclair Weeks.

government.

Greatly concerned with strengthening the defenses of the free world, Eisenhower labored for many months to set up an alliance of free nations in the Far East. He wanted this alliance to be comparable to NATO, the Atlantic mutual defense pact of the Western democracies. In September of 1954, this goal was partially

achieved when eight nations signed the Southeast Asia
Collective Defense Treaty at Manila. The eight mem-
bers that joined this Southeast Asia Treaty Organization
(SEATO) were Australia, France, Great Britain, New
Zealand, Pakistan, the Philippines, Thailand and the
United States.

Meanwhile on the domestic front President Eisenhower was building up the nation's defense establishment, dealing with the nagging problems of rising farm
surpluses and inflation, revitalizing the national economy,
and turning his attention to many other urgent matters.
His leadership for foreign aid to newly emerging countries and his liberal foreign trade policies drew fire from
some members of his own party. For the first year he
received the overall support of his party seventy-four
percent of the time. During his second year, in the
course of eighteen roll calls dealing with foreign policy,
the Democratic opposition in the Senate supported the
President more frequently than his own party. A new-
comer to politics, President Eisenhower found this
experience nettling.

The death of the Senate majority leader during
Eisenhower's first year in office was a most unfortunate
blow. Senator Taft was struck down by cancer the last
day of July, 1953, just as he and Ike had begun to
function effectively as a team in piloting administration
legislation through Congress. Taft had differed with the
President in matters of foreign policy, but he was a
deep believer in the ground rules of American politics
that recognized the president as captain of the team

when his party held the White House. He supported
Ike loyally. Taft's high prestige in the Senate was a
great factor in persuading some Republicans to go along
with the President's programs.

Midpassage in Eisenhower's first term, the Republicans
lost control of Congress. This defeat, added to Taft's
death, brought new burdens to the President. Meanwhile international tensions constantly threatened. Late
in 1952 the United States exploded the first hydrogen
bomb. A little more than a year later the experiment
was duplicated by Russian scientists. Soon England
successfully demonstrated her nuclear possibilities. War
by miscalculation had become an ever menacing possibility. For America the Atlantic and Pacific oceans
no longer offered a margin of safety as they had in
previous wars. Death and destruction were only minutes
away.

Deeply sensitive to this fearsome situation, Ike
had appealed publicly late in 1953 for extraordinary
measures to save mankind from a hydrogen war. Late
in 1954 he again said "that we owe it to ourselves and
the whole world to explore every possible means of
settling differences before we even think of such a thing
as war." Ike kept up the initiative. Soon the Russians,
who were also gravely disturbed about the consequences
of an atomic war, began making public statements on
the desirability of a disarmament conference.

The dramatic moment came at a Summit Conference
of the Big Four Powers in July of 1955, when Eisenhower without any previous notice put forth his "open

skies" proposal in a widely acclaimed speech. There were three major recommendations. First he called upon the Soviet Union and each of the other participants in the Conference to make available a complete blueprint of their military establishments. Next he asked that each of the nations provide facilities for aerial photography, so that regular air inspections could be made of each country's military bases. This would lessen the possibility of surprise attack. Finally he called for a comprehensive system of inspection and disarmament. It was one of Eisenhower's purposes to test by deeds, not words, the Soviet Union's professed desire to outlaw war.

The speech led to a long series of disarmament conferences, which continued even after he had left the White House.

On September 24th, two months after the Geneva conference, a distressing news flash was released from the summer White House headquarters at Lowry Field in Denver: The President had suffered a heart attack. A shocked country waited anxiously for further news.

During the several weeks Eisenhower spent at the hospital convalescing, his chief aide, Governor Adams, carried on the major burdens of the nation's business; and the Vice President, Richard Nixon, presided at National Security Council meetings. As Eisenhower regained his strength officials shuttled back and forth from the nation's capital to Denver to confer with the President.

Soon the leading question in domestic politics became: Will he run for president again? For several months Eisenhower brushed off all such queries with non-committal answers. He did say that this was a matter which he, his doctors, his family and his party would have to decide. And he promised that when the time arrived to make a proper evaluation he would give an answer. He also made it clear that if there were the slightest doubt of his being capable physically of handling the heavy responsibilities of the presidency, he would renounce a second term.

On February 29th, 1956, the long awaited word came: He would be a candidate, if the Republican party desired him as its nominee. His answer surprised some Washington veterans among the press, who had predicted he would not run again. But it had long been evident that Eisenhower's immense popularity had in no way sagged, either through the defeat of his party in the congressional elections of 1954 or because of his heart attack.

Just as events were shaping up nicely for Ike's renomination, and very likely his reëlection, a new crisis developed. This time it was a painful abdominal ailment known medically as ileitis. Seized by a critical attack in June of 1956, the President underwent surgery on short notice. Again the country pondered what effect this development would have on his political future. It had not long to wait. Emerging successfully from this bout of illness—his first words afterward were, "Oh what a bellyache"—Eisenhower convalesced rapidly and dispelled all doubts about running again for the presidency.

He was renominated at San Francisco's Cow Palace in August, 1956, with Nixon as his running mate. Once again his opponent was Adlai Stevenson, whom the Democrats had nominated earlier in the summer. That fall the broad campaign issues were peace, prosperity and Ike's surging popularity. A truce had finally been negotiated with the Communists in North Korea on July 27, 1953. And on the domestic front extensions of social security and old age benefits and the strengthening of civil rights for Negroes were all popular policies working on Eisenhower's behalf. Ike threw himself into the campaign with a vigor which gave no indication that he had suffered two serious illnesses. When the votes were tallied on November 6th, the results showed that he had won by a more impressive sweep than in 1952. He had carried forty-one states, with a popular plurality exceeding nine million votes. Moreover he carried some major American cities that his party had not won since 1920.

The Presidency and Its Aftermath

Though backed by a strong mandate from the people, Ike began his fifth year in office with many deeply disturbing problems. Through failure of his party to gain control of Congress, he started his second term with both houses of Congress in the hands of the opposition party. In Central Europe, he had inherited another crisis. Freedom-loving Hungarians had revolted against the autocratic rule of their leaders, hoping for support from their friends among the Western states. But Soviet tanks were sent to crush this revolt against tyranny, and help was not forthcoming from the West. Eisenhower urged the United Nations to condemn the intervention by the Soviets and the cruel suppression policies that were applied to put down the revolt. Nonetheless, resentment against the United States was high, not only among disappointed persons of Hungarian descent in this country, but equally among persons of Polish extraction and many other nationality groups who longed for the liberation of captive nations from Soviet domination in Eastern and Central Europe.

In the Middle East still another crisis erupted during the presidential campaign of 1956. This crisis brought the United States into a sharp conflict with two of its closest allies, England ʌand France. During July and

The President confers with his secretary of state, John Foster Dulles, before the latter flies to London to attend a 22-nation conference on the Suez Canal dispute.

August Egypt had nationalized the Suez Canal. In October England and France joined Israel in an invasion of Egypt. Eisenhower protested both of these actions, and the invaders eventually withdrew from Suez. But his stand against the position taken by England, France and Israel was much criticized in those countries and was highly unpopular with some groups in the United States.

Meanwhile in other areas of the Middle East tensions mounted because of continued Soviet efforts to agitate trouble within existing governments. In Lebanon intelligence reports indicated that an overthrow of the legal government with the help of Soviet influence might occur at any moment. Recognizing this danger, President Eisenhower appeared in person before Congress to ask for the adoption of policies that would increase the amount of economic aid to Middle Eastern countries and give the President authority to send military aid, if requested, in order to prevent domination of the area by an outside power. These policies, which Congress endorsed, were subsequently known as the Eisenhower Doctrine for the Middle East. Later the dispatch of American troops to Lebanon in support of those policies was generally hailed as a turning point in the test of wills. It proved that the United States was determined not to stand by idly while the Soviets sought to undermine legal governments in the Middle East.

Harassed by trouble spots in international affairs and the beginnings of an economic recession at home, Ike encountered yet another challenge to American leadership. This time it came from the world of Soviet science. On October 4, 1957, the Russians succeeded in placing a satellite in orbit. Called Sputnik I, this satellite symbolized a new era in the story of rising Soviet might. Abroad it was hailed immediately as evidence that the Soviet Union was overtaking the United States not only in scientific discovery but in technical capability as well.

In the United States a startled nation reacted violently. The American space program came in for some sober, constructive criticisms that proved most helpful. But a vast amount of the shouting was sharply political. For weeks the would-be experts were making irresponsible statements about rocket propulsion, payloads, and other highly scientific subjects about which they were ill-equipped to speak.

President Eisenhower took the outcries in his usual stride. He was quick to point out that prior to his taking office virtually nothing had been done to launch a space program in the United States. He also noted that in 1955, as a result of a conference of scientists to plan for a geophysical year in 1957, a suggestion had been made that the United States government undertake a modest program to speed up the study and exploration of outer space. He had met with his scientific advisers and a figure of twenty-two million dollars had been agreed upon as the sum to provide for such exploration. Until the time Sputnik was launched, said Ike, no one had urged that greater funds were required.

The President then came up with a program to accelerate outer-space research. This program called for much larger appropriations, but Eisenhower emphasized that such matters as lunar probes, space stations and other essential requirements for the exploration of outer space should not become a national obsession. They should not be allowed to over-shadow the other urgent problems here on earth—foreign aid and a healthy national economy. The United States must not fall into the error of trying to match every Soviet achievement.

In the midst of preparing for a December NATO conference and starting work on his annual State of the Union message, Eisenhower suffered his third major illness in two years. On November 25, 1957, he drove out to National Airport to greet the king of Morocco. Standing bareheaded in the rain and cold, he apparently became excessively chilled. Upon his return to the White House he suffered a mild stroke that affected his speech.

By noon the next day, however, the President was relaxing by painting with oils, and had sent for his brother Milton. He was still having difficulties in calling to mind certain words he wanted to use, but it was already clear that his brain had suffered no serious damage and that he was on the mend.

The President was well enough to participate in the NATO Conference in December, but he looked visibly tired on his return and there was continual speculation about his health. January brought Congress back to Washington, and the President had to make his State of the Union address, usually the most important speech of the year. Troubled here and there with his delivery, he still managed to turn in an impressive performance for which he was roundly applauded by members of both political parties. It was a tribute to the man "Ike" from the Democrats, many of whom were at odds with his political policies.

The year 1958, like 1957, brought some major disappointments to Eisenhower. Though his health continued to improve, a congressional investigation disclosed that his aide, Sherman Adams, had acted indiscreetly. Public opinion and some party leaders brought pressure to bear, forcing Adams' resignation. This was a hard blow, for Eisenhower had great faith in Adams' judgment and talent, and he was extremely reluctant to let him go.

As the fall congressional campaign warmed up, Ike took off on an extensive midterm tour that carried him from coast to coast. But he was traveling against some stiff headwinds. Although the national income was at an all time high, the country was in a recession. There was particular discontent among farm groups who opposed the Secretary of Agriculture's policies designed to restore a free market for agricultural products. Eisenhower hit back at his critics harder than ever before—particularly at those who contended that America had slipped as a first-class power and was behind in armaments, in the missile race and in the strength of her defense establishment.

When the election returns were in, the Republicans found they had suffered serious losses in both the House and Senate.

The spring of 1959 found Ike waging a stiff fight to keep his program for foreign aid from being chopped back in Congress. At the same time he had to answer those critics who suggested that the nation's military forces had been subordinated to a balanced budget, greatly weakening the national defense. In May the death of Secretary of State John Foster Dulles after a long bout with cancer saddened Ike greatly. No member of his official family was as close to him as "Foster," and to lose him from the bridge in the closing days of his administration required a difficult adjustment. But the President made it quickly.

By summer of 1959 an appreciable change could be sensed in the tone of communications between the Soviet Union and the United States. In August, Eisenhower called a special press conference and released the secret. He had invited Nikita Khrushchev, the Soviet Premier, to visit the United States, and the Soviet leader had accepted. It was essential, explained the President, that something be done to melt the ice in the relations between the East and West. After months of careful thought he had concluded this might be a way to start. Shortly before Khrushchev arrived in September, the President made a short television broadcast, urging people to receive the visitor courteously, even though they deeply opposed the Soviet system.

The visit was a sensational event. Khrushchev traveled from coast to coast, visiting steel mills, hog farms and supermarkets. He capped the ten-day visit with an hour-long television broadcast over all networks. He returned to Russia apparently much pleased with the experience, and with the assurance that President Eisenhower would visit the Soviet Union probably the following spring. A second Summit Conference was also projected.

Meanwhile plans were being readied for the greatest presidential odyssey in American history: a trip that would take Eisenhower to a dozen countries and bring an American president to Asia for the first time. The move astounded his critics. Instead of functioning at the slower pace of most lame-duck presidents in their last two years, Ike was putting on a burst of speed that delighted his admirers and dismayed his critics. The purpose of his travels was threefold: to promote peace, better understanding and good will.

Starting in Rome, where he visited the Pope, President Eisenhower journeyed to Turkey, Pakistan, Afghanistan and India on the first leg of the trip. Everywhere his reception was tumultuous. In Afghanistan particularly he was practically smothered by people trying to keep close to him. Tribesmen hurtled down hills in somersaults trying to reach his car, and others walked right through icy streams with their clothes on.

India, however, provided the most unforgettable welcome. For days men, women and children had poured into New Delhi, the capital, by overloaded buses, trains, camel carts; and hundreds of thousands had come by foot. Arriving at the airport just at sunset, Eisen-

Excited crowds bombard President Eisenhower and Indian Prime Minister Nehru with flowers during a wild ride through New Delhi.

hower began the wildest ride he had ever taken. He was in an open car with Prime Minister Nehru. The route to the government palace was a winding river of people, vehicles, carts of all descriptions and animals. Inch by inch the car crawled through a surging melee of tossed flower blossoms and cheers. Ike and Nehru ducked, and occasionally winced, as some of the heavier bouquets hit too hard. On the rear of the car bearing the two leaders, grim-lipped Secret Service men were clinging precariously to the bumper as they tried to keep the exuberant Indians from climbing into the car.

In each country Ike made speeches, in which the

basic theme was always peace, understanding and America's great eagerness to work side by side with these nations to help them better their living conditions. The trip lasted three weeks, and was an important factor in speeding the preparations for an extended journey to South America in February.

Back in Washington in early March, Ike plunged immediately into a long list of festering troubles. Among them were Cuba and Castro, and the increasingly disturbing indications of difficulties ahead with Soviet Premier Khrushchev. Still encouraged by his Asian and Latin American trips, however, Eisenhower gave orders to go ahead with plans for the visit to Russia and a trip to the Far East.

Already there were warning signs of a possible blowup in Soviet-American relations. For months there had been difficulties over disarmament and nuclear test ban negotiations, and Khrushchev seemed to be bent on exploiting the missile shot Lunik I, which had hit the moon. "Our flag is flying on the moon," he said. "Is this not enough to prove the superiority of communism over capitalism?"

At a press conference President Eisenhower was asked what he thought of such a statement. He snapped: "I think it's crazy." Unfortunately several correspondents thought he said: "I think *he's* crazy." This is the sort of misunderstanding that is always a source of danger in a press conference. In this case the official, released transcript carried the second version even though a check of the tape recording showed clearly that the President said "it's" instead of "he's."

Unhappily a climate of suspicion was beginning to develop even before the mid-May Summit Conference at Paris. Then, if any faint hopes still remained, they came down with a thud on May 5th. On that day the Soviet Premier disclosed that an American U-2 plane had been shot down over Soviet territory. He placed before the world photographic evidence of the wreckage of the plane, a description of the intelligence mission it was supposed to perform, and photographs of its pilot, who had been captured.

The State Department said at first that there was no authorization for the flight. In line with traditional policy, many in official quarters felt strongly that the President should be disassociated from any connection with an intelligence mission of this sort. But on May 11th Eisenhower publicly called intelligence activity "a painful but vital necessity" and said, "no one wants another Pearl Harbor." He admitted that U-2 flights had been going on for four years. He said he still expected to go to Russia, however; but his expectations were quickly destroyed by the Soviet Premier. Khrushchev said he would be mad to ask the Russian people to welcome a man who "sends espionage planes here."

The Summit Conference, scheduled to open on May 16th, seemed doomed to failure before it ever began. No one, however, expected Khrushchev to heap on President Eisenhower the abuse that he did. In an offensive manner he demanded that the President apologize publicly for the U-2 flights, punish those

Over a nation-wide television and radio hookup, the President addresses the people on the subject of the U-2 plane shot down over Russia.

responsible, and promise never to do it again. As a final barb he told the President not to come to Russia.

Eisenhower, keeping calm in the face of insufferable rudeness, told Khrushchev that the flights had been halted and would not be resumed. He said they had been conducted only because of Russia's refusal to join the Free World in exposing their armaments to full view. He also said that in order not to upset the conference he would negotiate with the Soviet Premier separately on the question of the flights.

Khrushchev would have no part of such a proposal. Thus the conference, which had at one time promised so much, ended quickly and frighteningly. Khrushchev continued to deliver a long harangue to two thousand newspaper men—some of whom booed.

When Eisenhower drove back to the American Embassy, there were red patches on his face and his eyes were blazing. Yet he never did explode, even within the security of his own staff. Back in Washington, he decided to report to the American people by television, beginning with a full review of the U-2 incident. He accepted full responsibility for the flight, pushing aside all the arguments of advisers who were against such a course.

The wisdom of his decision was widely criticized. Deploring it, one critic wrote: "For the first time in modern history, the head of a state declared personal responsibility for an act of espionage." For Eisenhower it could not have been otherwise. Trained by a lifetime's experience to assume responsibility, he was not going to change now, even if his actions didn't conform to precedent. He also felt that if he did not accept responsibility, he would reinforce an argument the Communists had long been trying to sell; namely, that the President was merely a pawn of warmongering American capitalists and that he didn't really know what was going on.

While columnists and politicians continued to debate the question, President Eisenhower left Washington on a Far Eastern tour. In the Philippines, where he was still remembered for his four years spent in building up the Commonwealth army, he was received as a returning son. Two million turned out in Manila—a throng even larger than the crowd at New Delhi. He had also planned to visit Japan, but a rise of anti-American feeling there caused the Japanese Cabinet to ask that the President postpone his visit. They feared that domestic disturbances, in addition to creating embarrassment, might threaten the very safety of the President. The head of the Secret Service was enormously relieved, and back in the United States everyone applauded the wisdom of the decision to cancel the visit.

Contemplating his almost two terms in the White House at mid-summer, 1960, President Eisenhower could look back on 318,000 miles of travel with visits to 27 nations. While personal diplomacy alone cannot dissolve the differences that divide men and nations, Ike's great efforts to radiate friendship unmistakably helped promote better understanding for the United States, especially in Asia and Latin America.

That same summer Eisenhower began what is always one of the most difficult phases of the presidency—the last lap before the duly elected successor formally takes over. Vice President Nixon was virtually unchallenged for the Republican presidential nomination, and once the Democratic party had nominated John F. Kennedy the duel was on. And a fierce one it was, ending in the closest contest (in popular votes) the nation had yet seen.

Whatever his private feelings at Nixon's defeat, Eisenhower quickly mobilized his staff for the smoothest possible transition to a new Democratic administration. As the weight of the presidency was about to lift from his shoulders, Ike was determined that there should be a gracious transfer of power. He even found some parts of the process amusing. Emerging on the north portico of the White House to greet President-elect Kennedy, he saw for the first time the sprawling wooden reviewing stand being erected on Pennsylvania Avenue for the inaugural parade. Suddenly the stern presidential frown broke into a big grin as he snapped: "I feel like the fellow in jail who is watching his scaffold being built."

January brought a flurry of farewells to old friends. It also brought lonely moments as big army trucks lumbered off into the darkness carrying cartons of papers and gifts from kings, sultans and the poor—on to the Eisenhower Museum at Abilene. And daily Ike turned to one special assignment close to his heart—his farewell address. Friends thought he should appear before Congress to deliver it. But Ike said no. It was the content that counted, he said, not the immediate contact. He was striving to reach tomorrow's conscience, not today's headlines.

On January 17, 1961, the oval office was invaded by the television cameras for the last time while Dwight D. Eisenhower was president. Maroon-colored felt was taped to his desk to cut the glare, and electric cables crisscrossed the floor like a bed of snakes. Ike began his short fifteen-minute address slowly. It was fifty years, he said, since he had entered the public service when appointed to West Point by a United States Senator. He was grateful to the nation and to the Congress which had coöperated with him throughout this half-century of America's adventure in free government. Then, after wishing his successor Godspeed and every good fortune, he jumped into his farewell theme.

Unlike her earlier years, he said, America had now been compelled to create a permanent armaments industry of "vast proportions." Over three and one half million men were in the service of the national military establishment alone. The coming together of this immense military establishment and a large arms industry meant that its combined influence—"economic, political, and spiritual"—would be felt in every city, state house, and every office of the federal government. The implications of such power were explosive. Because the possibility for the "disastrous rise of misplaced power exists and will persist, we must guard against the acquisition of unwarranted influence of the military-industrial complex within the councils of government."

The outgoing president said he wished he could report that a lasting peace was in sight, but happily he could say that war had been avoided. Then he closed with the simple remark that he was proud to soon become a private citizen.

Now in his seventieth year as he took leave of the presidency, Ike looked strangely unlike a departing Chief Executive on inauguration day. He still had the color and complexion of a healthy child. Bouncing about before the drive to the Capitol, with his pale, piercing-blue eyes taking in every last-minute detail, he stood out in marked contrast to many statesmen in both parties, far his junior in years. Late that day he returned to Gettysburg—back to the only home he and Mamie had ever owned in forty years of marriage.

Where will he rank in the hall of heroes? For the war years his great vision can only shine more brightly with the passage of time. His was the conception of an international staff in which the decisive loyalty would be to the institution itself. That this idea triumphantly prevailed was not just a matter of the Supreme Commander's bold concept of a unified command, but also his superb talent for getting men to pull together in harness. "I ran to Ike at least five times boiling with fury, cursing and screaming about Monty [Britain's General Montgomery]," wrote Prince Bernhard of the Netherlands in his *Memoirs*. "Ike always remained amazingly calm and correct. 'It is no good cursing him,' he said, 'He is doing his best and you are doing your best.'"

And once, after he had apologized for a misstatement, Ike confided to an old friend: "Let me tell you this.

In snow-covered Gettysburg, former President Dwight D. Eisenhower walks from his barn to his house—"the only home he and Mamie had ever owned."

Any man who is not prepared to admit publicly that he has been wrong is wrong." Then in a quieter voice he added: "I have made plenty of mistakes myself."

Here is the true measure of a man who wielded supreme power successfully, at times brilliantly, and laid it aside gracefully. This is why the thousands who knew him at close range and the millions who knew him only from afar but still felt his spell, will always rank him high in the long line of American heroes.

Index

About the author

MALCOLM MOOS was able to draw upon much first-hand information in writing this Landmark biography of Dwight D. Eisenhower. In 1957, during the Eisenhower Administration, Mr. Moos was appointed consultant in the White House Office and later he became Administrative Assistant to President Eisenhower.

A native of St. Paul, Minnesota, Dr. Moos received his A.B. and M.A. degrees from the University of Minnesota and was awarded his doctorate by the University of California. He has taught political science at the Universities of Minnesota, California, Wyoming, and Michigan, as well as at The Johns Hopkins University and Columbia University.

Dr. Moos began his writing career as associate editor of the *Baltimore Evening Sun*. He is the author of several books including *A Grammar of American Politics; The Republicans: A History of their Party; H. L. Mencken: A Carnival of Buncombe,* and *Hats in the Ring* (with Stephen Hess). He lives with his family in Tarrytown, New York.

U.S. LANDMARK BOOKS